Ten Moments That Changed Cricket

World's Youngest Sports Author

Hasan Malik

FEROZSONS (Pvt.) LTD.
LAHORE-RAWALPINDI-KARACHI

ISBN 978-969-0-02929-4

First published 2024 by
Ferozsons (Pvt.) Ltd.
81-D/1, Main Boulevard, Gulberg-III, Lahore
277, Peshawar Road, Rawalpindi
Mehran Heights, Main Clifton Road, Karachi

Malik, Hasan

Ten Moments That Changed Cricket

Published by
Zaheer Salam, Ferozsons (Pvt.) Ltd.,
81-D/1, Main Boulevard, Gulberg-III,
Lahore-54660, Pakistan

Printed in Pakistan at
Ferozsons (Pvt.) Ltd., (Printing Div.) Lahore.

email: support@ferozsons.com.pk
www.ferozsons.com.pk

*Dedicated to Mama Jani and Baba Jani
for being my biggest fans,
my biggest critics,
and my heroes.*

Table of Contents

Foreword by Ali Khan Tareen, Owner of the Multan Sultans . . . 7

Chapter One: The Origins of the Ashes 10

Chapter Two: Bodyline 22

Chapter Three: One Day, or Day One? 27

Chapter Four: Packer's Circus 37

Chapter Five: The 1992 World Cup 44

Chapter Six: 22 off 1 67

Chapter Seven: The Impossible Chase 77

Chapter Eight: The Boulder of Sisyphus 85

Chapter Nine: The Rise of T20 97

Chapter Ten: Franchise Leagues: A New World Order? 108

Epilogue: A New Dawn 121

About the Author

Hasan Malik is the world's youngest sports author. Running Pakistan's most popular youth sports blog, The Cricketing Hour, he analyses cricketing history, contemporary matches, and the rise of data analytics in sport.

The Cricketing Hour is a haven for cricket fanatics - dissecting the latest news in the world of cricket, previewing upcoming series and matches, and performing pre-match and post-match analyses of the biggest tournaments in the world of cricket. Lately, the blog has branched out via their YouTube channel, producing bilingual videos in both English and Urdu for greater accessibility, as well as releasing bite-sized YouTube Shorts for casual fans wanting quick recaps.

Hasan has also written about contemporary issues - such as the rise of T20 cricket and the decline of the red-ball format - in *The Minute Mirror*, a national newspaper. Furthermore, he has given talks about modern cricket on large-scale platforms, such as *MM Talks* in 2023.

Graduating from Aitchison College in 2024 - where he served as a Prefect and was declared the Best Declamation Speaker - Hasan is now pursuing Studies in Computer Science at the University of Toronto.

The author can be contacted at hasanmalik.office@gmail.com.

Foreword
by Mr. Ali Khan Tareen

Mr. Ali Khan Tareen is a businessman, philanthropist, and the owner of the Multan Sultans franchise in the Pakistan Super League.

During a PSL season, a friend sent me an Instagram post about a show called *The Cricketing Hour*. The depth and maturity of the host's analysis were far beyond anything I had encountered in recent times. I was so impressed that I immediately shared it with my team, and they were equally captivated. The person we were all impressed by was Hasan Malik. Since then, I have followed Hasan's work and career with great interest.

As a lifelong fan of cricket, it's a great honour to write the foreword for this book by someone so young and talented.

When Hasan told me about his project to capture the key moments that changed cricket, I was thrilled. As someone who has admired Hasan's ability to convey complex ideas and narratives in an accessible and engaging manner, I knew this book would be a treat for any reader.

"Ten Moments That Changed Cricket" is a must-read for all cricket fans, from the hard-nosed Test purists to the casual big-game watchers. Cricket is a game with a rich history spanning hundreds of years, and has evolved in ways that no other sport has. Like the pitches we play on, cricket grows and changes at will.

As fans, we sometimes fail to grasp the full impact of certain moments in cricket history. For example, a newspaper headline about England losing a series led to the naming of the most fiercely contested rivalry in Test cricket. A disgruntled Australian media mogul's failure to get cricket rights led to him starting his own tournament, which took cricket from white to technicolour. And who could forget the high-scoring ODI that resulted in the highest-ever team total, only to be chased down on the same day, forever changing our expectations of the theoretical limits of our sport?

T20 cricket was started as a bit of afternoon fun; it is now the biggest business cricket has known. Fundamentally altering the way cricket is played. Batters no longer have the luxury of taking time to settle in; instead, they aim to maximise the powerplay overs by scoring boundaries from the very start of their innings. This has led to the development of innovative shots that allow them to score runs all around the ground; including over their own heads. Bowlers, in turn, have adapted. Spinners bowl quicker; quicks bowl slower balls that spin.

The aggressive approach and innovative techniques pioneered in T20 cricket have also filtered into ODI and Test cricket. Players are now more willing to take risks, and teams aim for faster run rates, even in the longer formats. Traditional defensive batting and conservative strategies have become less prominent, with players often focusing on seizing momentum through aggressive play. A great example of this is the England cricket team, where the term "Bazball" has been coined to describe their recent free-flowing batting style in Test cricket.

Reading *Ten Moments That Changed Cricket* has deepened my understanding of cricket's evolution and the direction in which it is heading. The book arrives at a critical juncture when many are uncertain about the future of the sport. Will Test cricket expand to associate nations or contract to the so-called "Big Six"? With the ever-rising popularity of T20s, will ODIs survive? Will shorter formats like T10 or the controversial Hundred make a lasting impact? Will cricket make it to the Olympics permanently? And will the private franchise circuit eventually overshadow the ICC?

Only time will answer these questions. But by looking at the past, as Hasan so brilliantly does in this book, we can better prepare for the future.

Ali Khan Tareen,
A lifelong cricket fan

The Origins of The Ashes

What would tennis be without Wimbledon, or cycling without the Tour de France, or motorsport without Le Mans? In a similar vein, cricket without the Ashes would have been a dull and dry affair.

Every sport needs a rivalry to establish itself. Rivalries create narratives, build heroes, and draw crowds. Players' careers are defined by sporting rivalries: Chetan Sharma is not known for taking 67 splendid ODI wickets, but for conceding a last-ball six to Javed Miandad in the 1986 Australasia Cup Final. Nor is Sreesanth known for the 169 international wickets he took, but for one solitary catch at fine leg in the 2007 World T20 Final.

I do not intend to trivialise his splendid career - indeed, Sreesanth played crucial match-winning roles in many Tests, ODIs, and T20Is alike - but in the minds of many, he is simply the fielder who took the catch that ended a cricket-crazy nations' 24-year World Cup drought. He might as well have been a specialist fielder all his life.

It is well-documented that sportsmen run faster, hit harder, and jump higher in big games - World Cups, big finals, sporting rivalries and the like - than in other matches. They can talk as much as they like about "dealing with pressure" and it being "just like any other game", but it evidently isn't. Who could have envisaged Mike Gatting hitting an audacious reverse-sweep in 1987, except when the pressure of the biggest trophy in cricket got to him?

It is also well-established that, from a commercial perspective, nothing attracts audiences like a good old rivalry. The thrilling South Africa vs Sri Lanka Test at Durban, as Kusal Perera singlehandedly led his side to a one-wicket win, was no less a fairytale comeback than Ben Stokes' heroics at Headingley six months later. Yet, while 965,000 viewers saw the latter unfold live on Sky, the former remains relatively obscure to this day.

Thus, for any sport to be financially viable, it is a foremost priority to develop a strong and anticipated rivalry. As the rivalry grows, the sport becomes front-page news rather than third-page filler. More audiences start clocking in, more journalists start devoting it column space, and the game starts infiltrating more casual conversations at bars and coffee shops.

Cricket's watershed moment came in 1882 at The Oval.

International cricket had commenced well before this, when Canada toured the United States in September 1844, with the tourists emerging victorious in the sole match at New York. Following this, in 1859, England began dispatching international teams of cricketers to North America and Down Under; Australia reciprocated in 1868 by sending a team of Aboriginal cricketers to England for a six-month-long season of cricket - winning 14, losing 14, and drawing 19 matches. However, cricket was still irregular and infrequent.

In 1877, James Lillywhite's professional English team toured Australia, playing two games - winning one and losing one. We can already gauge, judging by the 1868 tour, that the two countries were fairly evenly-matched - a good omen for a sporting contest.

When Clarence P. Moody, the pioneer of Australian cricket journalism, wrote his treatise titled *"Australian Cricket and Cricketers, 1856 to 1893-94"*, he listed the 39 competitive matches that he considered worthy of being given "Test" status - beginning with the 1877 tour. The list became generally accepted, and to this day the first Test match is considered to be Australia's 45-run victory over England at the MCG. The first ball was bowled by Alfred Shaw to Charles Bannerman, and our sport burst out of its cocoon.

However, the wings of the butterfly were still not fully developed - not until 1882, when Australia, yet to win a single Test match in England, headed to the Oval for a lone Test.

Chasing 85 in the fourth innings on what was later described as a "sticky wicket", England were comfortable at 50/2, with the evergreen master of the wooden willow, W.G. Grace, still at the crease. Although a few words had been exchanged when Sammy Jones of Australia was run-out by W.G. Grace when he considered the ball to be dead (a controversy resurrected by Bairstow and Carey a hundred and forty-one years later, ironically with the Englishman being run-out this time), the match largely remained an England-dominated affair.

That is, until Fred "The Demon" Spofforth decided otherwise.

Bowling thirty-three maidens in the match, the Aussie pace-bowling spearhead resurrected the despairing tourists in the second innings. Famously declaring, "This thing can be done!" in the innings break, he immortalised his words by catalysing an English collapse from 66/4 to 77 all-out in the second essay, registering figures of 7/44 in the process. Harry Boyle took the crucial wicket of Sir W.G. Grace, the top-scorer for the hosts, as Australia stole a seven-run victory from the jaws of defeat.

Jack Worrall, writing for the Australian publication *Argus* in 1930, declared the match to be "one of the greatest in all cricket history." Indeed, the game was swiftly recognised as a classic, and the English press had a field day with the Oval upset.

Cricket: A Weekly Record of the Game, a British publication, produced an obituary of "England's supremacy in the cricket field, which expired on the 29th day of August... its end was Peate", mocking Ted Peate, England's No.11, who had refused to give strike to Charles Studd, the last-remaining recognized batsman at the non-striker's end when England's final wicket fell.

The Sporting Times, though, stole the show on the 2nd of September, when Reginald Shirley Brooks' infamous obituary appeared:

In Affectionate Remembrance

Of

ENGLISH CRICKET,

Which died at the Oval

On

29th August, 1882,

Deeply lamented by a large circle of sorrowing friends and acquaintances.

R.I.P.

N.B. - The body will be cremated and the ashes taken to Australia.

I need not explain the significance of the last line. For it was this very newspaper report that first coined the term "ashes" in the context of Anglo-Australian cricket. No doubt Brooks did not yet understand the significance of his word choice; he never fully would, as he passed away in 1888.

Nonetheless, the Australian victory was considered an upset, and preparations duly began in the England camp for the return tour in December 1882.

Let us return to the question of how the Ashes got their name. Credit must be given to Ivo Bligh, England's captain for the return tour; promising to avenge the Oval embarrassment, he referenced Brooks' obituary and stated his desire to "recover those ashes".

England subsequently won the series 2-1; afterwards, a Fourth Test was organised that ended up being won by the hosts, but the series is considered to have concluded after the initially-agreed-upon three Tests. Bligh is said to have referred to his goal to regain the "ashes" multiple times during the tour, no doubt playing a vital role in spreading the term.

After England's victory (or, depending upon which version of events you believe - the exact order is disputed - before the series began), a group of Melburnian women - notable among them was the wife of Sir W. J. Clarke, who had hosted the visiting team - presented Bligh with an urn, containing upon it the following iconic verses:

> *When Ivo goes back with the urn, the urn;*
>
> *Studds, Steel, Read and Tylecote return, return;*
>
> *The welkin will ring loud,*
>
> *The great crowd will feel proud,*
>
> *Seeing Barlow and Bates with the urn, the urn;*
>
> *And the rest coming home with the urn.*

This very urn was to become the single most iconic item of cricket imagery that the game has ever known. It is this urn that is branded in every piece of Ashes media, this very urn that is fought over biannually with the same fervour as in 1882 or stronger, and this very urn that is gazed upon by awestruck visitors to the MCC Cricket Museum till this day.

There is some dispute as to the exact contents of the urn - whether it contains the ashes of a cricket bail, as claimed by Bligh's spouse in 1930, or, as claimed by Bligh's elderly daughter-in-law in 1998, the ashes of her mother-in-law's veil. Personally, due to the temporal proximity of the 1930 claim to the actual presentation of the urn to Bligh, I am inclined to believe that the ashes belong to a cricket bail - a sentiment echoed by an MCC official during the 2006-07 Ashes.

However, leaving technicalities aside - finally in 1882, cricket could claim it had a rivalry on its hands.

Though it was a while before the term "the Ashes" became widespread, the fire had been lit under the England/Australia tours. Spofforth and Bligh, along with Grace, Boyle, and the rest, had each given their fans something to cherish. England enjoyed an initial period of dominance as it won all Ashes series till 1896 bar one; the 1894-95 iteration in particular was a hotly-contested one, featuring a come-from-behind England victory after following-on, and eventually concluding 3-2 in England's favour. The balance of power would tilt from England to Australia and back again continuously until today: Australia have won the series 34 times to England's 32, with 7 drawn series (resulting in the previous winner retaining the Ashes).

Let us now take a look at the impact of the establishment of the Ashes.

> **"Finally in 1882, cricket could claim it had a rivalry on its hands."**

Firstly, player quality increased massively. In 1890, England established the County Championship, aiming to discover and develop its finest young cricketers to be used as weapons in the Ashes series. This also made cricket a far more financially-viable career path for budding youngsters, as eight clubs were officially recognised to compete in the Championship. Subsequently, cricket rapidly grew in England, and they maintained their early stronghold over Australia.

The Aussies, however, did not lag far behind; their own domestic red-ball league, the Sheffield Shield, was set up in 1892, and they began chipping into England's headstart on the Ashes. When the Proteas and New Zealand joined cricket, they too followed in England's footsteps, setting up the Currie Cup and Plunket Shield respectively to hone young talent. India later established the Ranji Trophy, and the trend of domestic leagues remains to this day. Nonetheless, the Ashes was a key motivator for England and Australia to start investing more in their future stars.

Secondly, both countries needed regulatory boards to start managing players, logistics, and finances, as well as liaising with other international teams and scheduling fixtures. The England team was run by the Marylebone Cricket Club (MCC) from 1903 onwards, and the Australians formed an Australian Board of Control for International Cricket in 1905. These boards helped decide player salaries, match venues, and squad selection.

Another consequence of this was the founding of the ICC. The President of the South African Cricket Association, Abe Bailey, deserves the lion's share of the credit for this endeavour: in 1907, he proposed an "Imperial Cricket Board" to be formed, to govern a tripartite championship between the three Test-playing nations.

His revolutionary vision was not shared by his British and Australian counterparts, and the idea consequently fell through;

nonetheless, during Australia's tour of England in 1909, he was able to call a meeting of representatives from all three cricket boards, who then agreed to form the Imperial Cricket Conference - later renamed the International Cricket Council in 1964.

It is interesting to note here that the rules of cricket initially agreed-upon included some stark differences from the ones we are currently used to. For one, the number of balls in an over was not standardised to six; indeed, cricket was born with mere four-ball overs, that became five in 1889 and grew to six in 1900. However, the stubborn Australians stuck with eight-ball overs late into the seventies, as Law 17.1 had left it up to the two captains to agree upon the number of balls per over before the toss. It was only in 1980 that six balls per over became the Law.

Similarly, fielding restrictions were not yet developed - indeed, the absence of the thirty-yard circle is conspicuous in old cricketing pictures - and British tacticians unabashedly exploited this loophole in the 1932-33 Bodyline series. The LBW ruling was also different: it was mandatory for the ball to pitch in line for an LBW dismissal, which ended up being relaxed in 1937 to allow the ball to pitch outside off, as we are nowadays accustomed to.

Lastly, it would be a crime to discuss this portion of cricketing history without discussing the spread of cricket in other countries.

You will recall that the first international match was played between USA and Canada in 1844 - an odd piece of trivia, as neither of these two teams, to this day, have achieved Test status. At the time, cricket was also rampant in Mexico and Netherlands - again, two countries that have not achieved Test status till today.

It pains me to say this, but there is no denying the fact that the ICC's lack of vision and ambition squandered what was essentially a fifty-year headstart on football in terms of spreading the game.

While the game was a colonial pastime that the British spread in all their colonies - and South Africa, New Zealand, and India all consequently became Test-playing nations by the 1930s - the game was still considered to be one for the elite. Cricket remained primarily restricted to upper-class clubs, as not everyone could afford the gear needed to bat and bowl, nor were suitable pitches available except after careful curation. By contrast, kicking a football around hardly demands any financial expenditure. The duration of multi-day cricket matches - T20 wasn't a thing back then - was undoubtedly another hurdle that gave football the advantage.

However, when British influence began to decline - notably after World War 1, when many wealthy British expats returned home, and especially after the Mexican Revolution in Latin America - cricket had no guardian left, and the clubs were swiftly replaced by the growing epidemic of football.

"There's a real similarity with Denmark and the Netherlands and other countries where cricket arrived early but remained among the elites," remarked Craig White, secretary of the Mexico Cricket Association, speaking to the Guardian in 2021. "It was a missed opportunity – cricket had a head start on football and baseball by at least half a century and it was squandered."

Similarly, as British influence in America waned, so too did interest in cricket.

It is imperative for the reader to understand that, unlike today, playing cricket was seen as an intrinsically *British* act. Nowadays, no sport carries such a nationalistic touch, which makes it harder for us to grasp this concept. Colonised folk would often - seeking to establish good favour with their British overlords - try to establish good rapport with their colonisers; the cricket clubs, being lounges for the aristocrats and the ruling elite, naturally became the perfect place to do so. The Brooklyn Eagle, an American publication, stated in 1862: "Cricket is essentially an English game; a game in such favour with the English cannot well have much attraction for the American, the disposition of both people being as different as baseball is from cricket." This shows the nationalistic weight playing cricket carried in the minds of the Americans. The American Civil War in the 1860s further pushed the sport to the peripheries of the American imagination, and as British expatriates began leaving the US in the late 19th and early 20th centuries, American cricket subsequently declined.

In 1855 - well before the dawn of the Ashes - the New York Clipper had estimated the number of active cricketers in America to be over 5000. Why, then, did cricket lose out to baseball?

"There is no denying the fact that the ICC's lack of vision and ambition squandered what was essentially a fifty-year headstart on football in terms of spreading the game."

While cricket's mandatory monetary investment and lengthy duration were undoubtedly responsible factors - the New York Times wrote in 1859 that American players were "unable to spare more than a few leisure hours a week from their offices" - blame must be levelled on a lack of coordination between English and Australian players and their American counterparts.

While England and Australia - with two oceans between them - could regularly tour one another throughout the latter half of the 19th century, they remained uninterested in dealing with the American cricket fraternity. Partially, this was because of the perceived lack of quality in American cricket: when George Parr's English team toured Canada and the United States in

September and October 1859, they crushed the hosts convincingly in every single game they played. Nonetheless, it is likely that future tours would have occurred had the American Civil War not begun immediately afterwards, and when the British returned in 1868, they found baseball to have eclipsed cricket's popularity.

The ICC is not innocent either.

Why, as soon as it was formed in 1909, its first priority should have been to rescue the remaining cricketing circles in Canada, the United States, Mexico, etc. Yet the ICC's abject obstinacy, inaction, and lack of ambition prevented non-Commonwealth nations from entering the sport. The ICC is guilty of making no attempt towards any contact with American cricket all the way until 1965, when it added the USA as an Associate member.

And now, watching the ICC restlessly chase acceptance in American circles, one cannot help but marvel at the open-goal it missed a century ago.

Having half a World Cup in the States is a good start, sure, but sowing the seeds a hundred years earlier would doubtless have culminated in a healthier harvest.

Why, the 1912 Triangular Series could have been a multilateral affair with Canada, Mexico, and the USA all being invited. Let them be uncompetitive - South Africa didn't exactly light the stage on fire either - but let them join! Gatekeeping the sport in the first half of the 20th century was undoubtedly the biggest blunder the ICC will ever have the chance to make.

Indeed, the decision to let the Caribbean islands merge together to form one unified cricket team - the West Indies - is one of the only pragmatic decisions the ICC took in this time period - and that too only after more than thirty years of disparate Caribbean cricket. Denmark, too, could have been a haven of cricket -

having more than thirty cricket clubs by 1883 alone - yet remained unrecognized by the ICC until 1966!

Yes, the Ashes was - and is - a fantastic rivalry.

But why did it take 217 Test Matches for the first game not involving either England or Australia to be played?

Why did the ICC seek to shut its doors, rather than open them wide?

Why was the ICC content with the Ashes alone, when we could have had a fierce rivalry between Canada and the USA, a superlative struggle between the Danes and the Dutch, and an almighty clash between the Mexicans and the Brazilians?

Indeed, the tale of the origins of the Ashes is nothing but a tragic reminder of the opportunities cricket missed out on: the rivalries we will never know.

Bodyline

Rarely has there been such a defining moment in a sport's history as the Bodyline series has been for cricket. It marks the first generational divide of cricket: Is it a sport, or a profession? Is it "win at all costs", or "win with grace"? Or, to phrase it in a more contemporaneous way, is the Spirit of Cricket more important than the word of its Laws?

These questions were the ones that faced Douglas Jardine and his English team on their 1932-33 tour of Australia. Having been terrorised by Donald Bradman's 974 runs at an average of 139.14 in the previous Ashes, they sought to come up with a plan to counter his prolific play.

Jardine, the skipper, alongside his fearsome pacers Harold Larwood and Bill Voce, and former England captain Arthur Carr, devised the infamous tactics we now recognise as "Bodyline". When he observed Bradman's struggles against short-pitched fast bowling via video footage of the Oval Test in 1930, Jardine had his Eureka moment. He felt that he had deciphered the myth of how to conquer Bradman. Why, if the leg-side field were packed with fielders, and two relentless pacers could consistently pitch the ball short on leg-stump, the batsmen would have no choice but to play into the hands of the waiting leg-side fielders! The puzzle fit together perfectly!

Or so, atleast, thought Jardine.

When Bodyline was first tried in the lead-up to the Ashes series, it led to a furore among Australian crowds. Larwood in particular was mightily effective: his pacy balls zipped around the surface, beating Australian batsmen's pulls and occasionally barging into their bodies. When Bradman opted out of the first Test, Jardine's eyes lit up - and rightfully so, for England took a dominating victory as Larwood piled up match figures of 10/124.

In a first-class game against New South Wales, Bill Voce used these short-pitched tactics to dismiss Australian batsmen for low scores. Only Jack Fingleton stood up with a hundred, but even he was peppered by continuous blows to his upper body. The controversy mounted - the tactics were effective, sure, but were they safe?

The fire picked up fuel in the second Test, when Bradman was dismissed for a duck in the first innings. Although he scored an unbeaten century to lead Australia to victory, countering Larwood's Bodyline bowling on a relatively placid pitch, questions remained regarding the tactics' safety.

Those questions redoubled in intensity after the notorious Third Test at Adelaide. On a bouncy wicket, Larwood bowled with the new ball to the Aussie skipper, Bill Woodfull, narrowly missing his head in the third over. Remember - these were the days before batting helmets were in use! The next ball struck Woodfull smack on the chest, and he stumbled in agony. Soon after, another delivery knocked the bat out of his hands before he was dismissed for a painful 22.

This was the spark that ignited the fire. Aussie spectators jeered and shouted at the English fielders, clearly dismayed by what they felt was a blatant disregard for the Spirit of Cricket. Many were disgusted by the violent tactics of Jardine's men, while others remained adamant that it was permitted in the Laws of Cricket at the time.

"The tactics were effective, sure, but were they safe?"

While England went on to dominate the series, winning the series 4-1 - which remains one of their most successful campaigns in Australia - the MCC (Marylebone Cricket Club, the organisation responsible for the Laws of Cricket) now had a dilemma on its hands. Initially, it had authorised Bodyline after the events of the Third Test, but administrators remained uneasy, and eventually the MCC outlawed "direct attack" bowling, leaving it to the discretion of the umpires to identify and halt such bowling.

In modern cricket, Bodyline is simply illegal, due to the restriction on having more than two fielders behind square on the leg-side. Moreover, the addition of protective gear such as helmets further equips batsmen to counter leg theory bowling. However, the questions posed by this controversial series are still relevant to this day.

Firstly, the Bodyline series defines the marker between the times when cricket was a noble sport, played by gentlemen, and when cricket became a serious profession, a game played by those eager to win and ply their trade. Douglas Jardine could never have formulated his leg theory tactics in the 1890s or 1900s; cricket was not yet as mature or professional. The formation of the Imperial Cricket Council (the forerunner to the International Cricket Council) as well as various countries' cricket boards solidified its status as a professional sport. Thus, the stakes became higher, which engendered a "win at all costs" mentality, without which Bodyline would never have been possible.

Secondly, the series was a wake-up call for the administrators. It showed that they needed to have strict, well-controlled guidelines on what was permitted and what was illegal. Players were now much more willing to steal any inch of advantage whenever they had a sniff of an opportunity. When the MCC initially attempted to curb Bodyline, they passed a resolution declaring such tactics to be outside the Spirit of Cricket. However, this declaration completely fell flat, and it was not until Bodyline was outlawed that the captains finally desisted.

Thirdly, however, it renewed spectator interest in the sport. When Australia and England clashed in the Fourth Test of the 1932-33 Ashes, it was not merely a question of which team would win a meaningless sporting contest - rather, it was now the determinant of national pride, the answer to a question of cricketing ethics, and the solution to a puzzle of whether or not Australia could overcome England's newfound trump card. These narratives boosted the status of cricket as a nationwide sport, and indeed, it is not a coincidence that more than 63,000 Australians filled the MCG to watch Bradman take on Bodyline.

Most importantly, however, it was a statement by the English team that they were prepared to stop at nothing in their pursuit of victory. Only a similar determination to win at all costs could hope to compete with such a mindset. And, within a decade, the gloves were off, and all cricket teams were battling with the same ferocity.

The Bodyline series harks one back to simpler times, when extending the limits of what was allowed in the rules was frowned upon. How, one wonders, would the critics of Bodyline have reacted to India's usage of severely spinning pitches in 2015-16 to torment South Africa? Or how, perhaps, would they have lambasted the various cases of ball-tampering that have occurred? Even more egregiously, what would their verdict be on the cases of match-fixing, such as Cronje's infamous incident?

Frankly, if the Bodyline series happened in today's hyper-competitive world, no one would bat an eye. But in the cricketing atmosphere of the 1930s, it was a stratospheric calamity, an inconceivable crime.

It was the moment when cricket burst out of its cocoon, and realised its players were not always going to be gentlemanly. It destroyed the myth that teams and captains would not be eager to capitalise on any loophole in the rules.

"Frankly, if the Bodyline series happened in today's hyper-competitive world, no one would bat an eye."

Strangely enough, the same debate still occurs today. Those who once defended Bodyline are now those who argue in favour of the 'Mankad' mode of dismissal (running out the batsman at the non-striker's end), while the critics of Bodyline have now taken the shape of the Mankad's opponents.

While there are some differences between the two debates, the central conflict is the same: the word of the law as opposed to the spirit of cricket. While the former is objective and unforgiving, the latter is subjective and gregarious; while both Bodyline and the run-out at the non-striker's end are objectively legal, their spirit is still questioned.

Perhaps the Mankad will soon have its Bodyline moment: a controversial dismissal to decide a World Cup? A narrow run-out in a deciding Ashes Test? A one-run triumph, courtesy a Mankad, in a nail-biting IPL Final?

Whatever the case, the debate that was started by Bodyline lingers on today. And were it not for that notorious series, cricket would never have come of age as a competitive sport.

One Day, or Day One?

"Five whole days?"

"Yes - and often it's still not enough!"

Above is a conversation that any cricket tragic can relate to: dealing with the shocked exclamations of those who have not yet experienced the breathtaking beauty of Test cricket. First comes the astonishment, then the denial, and finally the sheer disbelief that people actually watch this game. Oh, if only they knew!

However, disregarding these petty folk, the question they raise is valid. Indeed, the administrators of English cricket found themselves dealing with the same challenge in the early sixties - how could cricket be made more decisive and fast-paced?

"By the early 60s, we had reached the end of cricket 's post-war boom," felt Mike Turner, the Leicestershire secretary at the time, and one of the pioneers of one-day cricket, speaking to ESPN Cricinfo. "The crowds had declined and there was a need to make the game viable. These were perilous times and there were arguments about which direction the game should take."

The MCC - encouraged by Turner - decreed for a knock-out style tournament of fast-paced, bite-sized one-day matches to be played between the counties in 1963. The goal was simple: attract crowds and bolster revenue. The rules were novel: each side would have 65 six-ball overs to bat, and each game would take no longer than a day. Gillette, the American safety razor company, agreed to sponsor the event, and the competition was christened "The First Class Knock Out Competition for the Gillette Cup" - a comically-lengthy name for cricket's "bite-sized" format.

Turner, however, was still not satisfied.

Seeing some gaps in Leicestershire's 1962 fixture list, Turner - ever an enterprising fellow - decided to get one-day cricket up and running. Contacting a few other counties who also had gaps in their schedule, he arranged for a four-team championship to be played in early May, 1962. Terming it a "dry run" for the 1963 Gillette Cup, he later remarked: "I saw some gaps in the fixture list and phoned around. My opposite numbers jumped at the chance." Turner's audacity did not end there; he swiftly arranged a broadcasting deal for the event and avariciously repolished a second-hand cup to be used as a winners' trophy: an ironic precursor to how future boards would use limited-overs cricket as a mere money-making machine.

Named the Midlands Knockout Competition, this humble three-match tournament was the first moment in cricketing history that a game was played with a limited number of overs per innings (65 at the time) - a concept that would revolutionise the very fundamentals of the sport.

It was also the first time that fielding restrictions were imposed: though there was still no concept of a "thirty-yard circle" or a "batting powerplay", there could be no more than six fielders on the off-side or five on the leg-side. Adding to this, captains were further challenged by the limit on the number of overs a bowler could deliver in an innings: fifteen at the time. These ideas were completely novel, and as Leicestershire and Derbyshire played out the first-ever one-day humdinger - a slender seven-run victory for Leicestershire - ODI cricket emerged from its nest and was ready to fly.

Although rain prevented large crowds from attending the matches, the response from the players was extremely positive, and Turner was delighted. The next year, the Gillette Cup proved to be a success - and before you knew it, one-day cricket became a staple in the domestic English circuit.

However, the ICC was - as always - slow in the uptake. Indeed, for the next decade, the ICC showed no desire to incorporate any semblance of one-day cricket into the international game - not until its hand was forced.

"However, the ICC was - as always - slow in the uptake."

The watershed moment came in 1971 at the MCG: poetically, the same ground where the first Test was played. After the first four days of the third Ashes Test were rained out, the officials - not wanting to disappoint the crowd of 46,000 hopefuls that had turned up - hastily arranged for a forty-over game to be played on the fifth day. (Remember, Australia still used eight-ball overs - the match would have 320 balls per innings.)

The MCC and ACB agreed to the game, and the players walked out for the first-ever One-Day International: just like the inaugural Test, an England/Australia affair, just like the inaugural Test, played at the MCG, and just like the inaugural Test, won by the home team in fairly convincing fashion.

However, the crowd was delighted.

"Terrific. If they played cricket all the time like this, they'd pack the M.C.G. No risk," remarked one of the spectators after the game, recorded by Ben Whitington. "You can't tell me there's any less skill involved. I'd reckon there's more skill."

Nearly a year and a half passed before the next ODI was played, this time on English shores as Australia played a three-match series following the Ashes. In 1973, Pakistan and New Zealand played a lone ODI, and within a year, West Indies and India too joined the ranks (South Africa, at the time, was exiled due to apartheid.)

Despite all these advancements in the sport, the ICC was still remarkably obstinate about organising a global tournament.

While football, basketball, and hockey - all with federations younger than, or contemporaneous to, the ICC - had established their own global tournaments in 1930, 1950 and 1971 respectively, the ICC displayed a remarkable lack of foresight and vision in conducting cricket's premier championship. Even a game as niche as chess had enjoyed regular World Championships throughout the 20th century - not so cricket!

Admittedly, cricket was a five-day affair unlike its rival sports, but conducting a knock-out tournament, akin to tennis, would surely have enabled a month-long tournament to take place. A round-robin could be played between the final four and the entire Cup would be wrapped up within a month and a half! The problem was not one of logistics, but of ambition.

However, with the dawn of ODI cricket, the logistical hurdles undoubtedly eased. Shockingly, though, the ICC still did nothing to capitalise on the opportunity. It was only a matter of time before someone took advantage of the situation, and before you knew it, cricket's first World Cup was conducted - not, however, by the ICC.

At the time, the ICC only governed the men's game; the International Women's Cricket Council, a wholly unrelated organisation founded in 1958, oversaw the women's game.

England's captain at the time, Rachel Heyhoe-Flint, was a

gamechanger in every sense of the word. With the bat, she was destructive - as the Australians found out in the inaugural World Cup Final. With her personality and words, she was no less adept, securing funding for multiple women's cricket tours in the '60s and '70s. A revolutionary captain, she was known for never losing a single match during her 12-year tenure as the English Test skipper. The first-ever woman to hit a six in Test cricket, Heyhoe-Flint set the record for the highest individual score in women's Tests in 1976, scoring a marathon 179* across eight-and-a-half hours as she secured a seemingly-improbable draw for her team. Scyld Berry, the renowned English analyst, called her the "Dr. WG Grace of women's cricket – the pioneer without whom the game would not be what it is." Almost as an aside, she was an integral player for the English hockey team, serving as the goalkeeper in 1964.

Over the years, Heyhoe-Flint developed a strong association with Jack Hayward, the British millionaire; persuaded by Heyhoe-Flint, Hayward financed several tours of the English women's cricket team, at a time when the women's game was severely under-financed. Having shown to Hayward that women's cricket was worth investing in, she proposed her most-ambitious idea to him in 1971: a global championship of women's cricket.

Heaven knows how she did it, or where cricket would be without her: Hayward agreed to finance the tournament, contributing a whopping sum of £40,000 for the first-ever Women's Cricket World Cup, hosted by the WCA (Women's Cricket Association, the governing board of women's cricket in England). Overseen by the International Women's Cricket Council, and won fittingly by Heyhoe-Flint's England outfit against their arch-rivals Australia, cricket's first-ever World Cup was a booming success - ironically, not conducted by the unambitious ICC.

It is worth lambasting here the role of the WCA. After Heyhoe-Flint's success, political tensions grew between her and the board; as a result, she was unceremoniously sacked as captain in 1978. Rather than utilising her celebrity status to further advance the popularity of the women's game, petty politicking proved to be an impasse; nonetheless, the World Cup had been established, which the IWCC - later to be merged with the   ICC in 2005 - continued to conduct every five years.

At any rate, the ICC had now truly been put to shame. The far-smaller-yet-far-bolder women's game had outshone the century-old men's sport, and the ICC finally decided to do what it ought to have done atleast twenty years earlier: the first-ever Cricket World Cup was held in 1975.

The venue was, again, England - the bastion of cricket, and the site of the successful 1973 women's edition. The Prudential Assurance Company became the title sponsors with a contribution of £100,000 - more than double Hayward's donation - and the six Test-playing nations competed against the top two Associate teams (Sri Lanka and an East Africa conglomerate).

The tournament featured standard ODI rules - 60 six-ball overs - and was two weeks long, featuring 15 matches. However, the first game of World Cup history remains undoubtedly the most (in)famous.

Smashing 334 against an Indian team struggling to adapt to the limited-overs format, England arrived with a bang. Sunil Gavaskar, the legendary subcontinental opener, though, remained utterly nonplussed. He strode out and proceeded to score a brisk 36 off 174 balls - still the slowest innings in World Cup history.

To this day, analysts are at a loss of words to explain his innings; the simplest explanation, however, is likely the most accurate. Gavaskar, conceding that 335 was a nigh-impossible target, simply treated the match as an extended practice session to get used to the bouncy British conditions. India ended the game at 132/4, comfortably losing the game by 202 runs.

However, this game was made up for by West Indies and Pakistan - arguably cricket's premier rivalry in the 70s and 80s. Chasing 268 for victory, the Windies were tottering at 203/9 before a heroic last-wicket stand took them home; Andy Roberts, the man who hit the memorable winning runs, speaking to Bharat Sundaresan in 2019, called it "the partnership that won us the World Cup." Similarly, an Australian side crippling at 39/6 against England in the semi-final limped to victory as they chased down 94 on a tricky wicket. The stage was set, the finalists decided: West Indies would face Australia in the first World Cup Final.

The final was an exciting affair, with the writer Norman Preston going on to declare: "It might not be termed first-class cricket, but the game has never produced better entertainment in one day." He further recorded: "The full attendance was 26,000 and the paying crowd produced receipts of £66,950, a record for a one-day match in England," outlining the tournament's commercial success.

Clive Lloyd, West Indies' visionary skipper, led the way with a blistering 85-ball ton: a fast-paced knock even by today's standards, and an otherworldly innings by theirs. Rohan Kanhai gave him ample support with a sturdy half-century, and the Windies posted 291 - barring the first match, the highest score of the tournament against a Test-playing team.

Deryck Murray, the West Indian wicket-keeper, later recalled, "Rohan Kanhai has never really received the kind of credit as he should for his innings. His score was only 55 in comparison to Lloyd's century but the influence he had at that particular time after we'd lost two wickets and Lloyd came in was enormous." Speaking to Cricbuzz, he added: "He steadied the ship. He provided the security for Lloyd to play his natural game."

Australia, though, were a batting powerhouse; the West Indian pace attack would be hard put to scythe a way through their top order.

A speedy little youngster by the name of Vivian Richards, though, had other ideas: in the biggest game of his blossoming career, he effected three run-outs - all of top four batters! - to shock the Aussie stalwarts. The Aussies were soon down and out at 233/9, before a 41-run stand between Lillee and Thomson threatened to steal the show. Deryck Murray, though, ever the cool-headed fellow, got the final breakthrough to seal the Cup with 17 runs in hand - and West Indies were crowned cricket's first kings.

"We didn't feel like world champions. The impetus was on Test cricket. ODI cricket was more a spectacle," recounted Andy Roberts, one of the victorious eleven, in 2019 to Cricbuzz. "There wasn't much celebration after the initial presentation."

"We didn't feel like world champions. The impetus was on Test cricket."

Deryck Murray, his compatriot who sealed the Final, echoed his sentiments: "While it was nice to be claimed as world champions around the cricket world, and our spectators did take great pride in that, they also wanted us to do that at the Test level."

Cricket - and more generally, sport - was still not fully out of its cocoon yet. Pre-match preparation, data analysis, and opponent-specific match-ups were all tactics that would develop gradually, as would the fanfare and ostentation of today. "There was no elaborate preparation like now," said Andy Roberts. "As a matter of fact, I left straight from Hampshire and went to join up with the team. I don't even remember if there was an opening ceremony. I believe we went to Buckingham Palace, all the teams."

However, the bottom line: the 1975 Prudential Cricket World Cup was a brilliant success. The spectators, players, and money-makers all loved the spectacle; the tourney was repeated in 1979 at the same venue and became a quadrennial event. The 1987 edition was the first to be held outside England, and by 1996, the six iterations had yielded five different winners (England, who ironically had won the inaugural women's World Cup, would not go on to win the men's tournament until the twelfth attempt).

Let us now discuss the impacts of the establishment of cricket's premier tournament.

Firstly, it was a means of filling the financial coffers of the ICC, and still is: the *Economic Times* estimated the ICC's revenue from the 2023 iteration to be $719 million, a colossal figure. Secondly, a World Cup gave cricket recognition: any sport's premier tournament acts as a natural entry point to attract new fans. Countless casual fans who don't follow football year-round will still check in to World Cup games; similarly, many who are not basketball fanatics or tennis tragics will still tune in to the NBA Finals or the Wimbledon Finals with great interest. Cricket, too, achieved the same goal with its World Cup: the 1983 edition in particular, won by India, sent the subcontinent into a cricketing frenzy that still lasts today.

Moreover, the mindset of every team changed in 1975: rather than simply play series amongst themselves, they now had a pinnacle to aim for. To this day, ODI cricket tends to have four-year cycles: aged legends retire after every World Cup, to allow the "next generation" to come in and start preparing for the next edition; players are dropped, coaches are changed, and tactics are renewed after each World Cup cycle, keeping the impending edition in mind; often, we see team philosophies radically change between World Cup cycles - the England team in 2014 was nothing like the England of 2015, as they embraced a new, more aggressive approach for the 2015-19 World Cup cycle. Articles are written, analyses are done, and statisticians analyse ODI cricket based on the trends between World Cup cycles. Inadvertently, the ICC had created a new measurement system of time by launching the Cricket World Cup.

Additionally, the quality of cricket went up a notch with the advent of World Cups. Ben Jones and Nathan Leamon, in their 2021 book, *Hitting Against the Spin,* note [emphasis added]: "At the World Cup, the average distance per match that players sprinted at high-intensity speeds (>20 kph) was *double the average distance* covered at those speeds in a typical ODI." This is but one example of how players pushed themselves to ever-greater heights at World Cups - consequently, the Cricket World Cup became a vehicle that raised the standard of cricket higher across the globe.

Some of the most iconic moments in world cricket - the 1992 semi-final, the 1999 Edgbaston tie, the 2019 Super Over - came in World Cups.

Undoubtedly, the advent of the one-day format and the subsequent establishment of the World Cup changed the game of cricket. From the classy whites, wooden bats, and defensive strokeplay of the early 1970s, ODI cricket - propelled by the incentive of winning a World Cup - became a haven of brightly-coloured uniforms (and dare I say, sponsor-littered jerseys), technological innovations (chiefly data analytics, stronger bats, and revolutionary broadcasting techniques), and totals surpassing 400 with ease.

Packer's Circus

Rarely is a businessman remembered less for his trade than his contributions to a sport. But then again, Kerry Packer was not an ordinary man at all.

The eccentric Australian was the first to discover the unexploited financial goldmines lying dormant in cricket, and the first to take advantage. Being the owner of the Nine Network, one of Australia's largest television channels, he innocently sought the rights to broadcast Australia's international cricket matches, but was repeatedly rebuffed by the Australian Cricket Board in deference to the Australian Broadcasting Corporation.

This was to be the domino that catalysed a series of events that shook the world of cricket - nay, sport globally. Higher pay for cricketers, batting helmets, coloured uniforms, night cricket under floodlights, drop-in pitches, franchise leagues, aggressive marketing campaigns, cricket-centric theme songs: all these phenomena which we take for granted in modern cricket originated when Kerry Packer decided to go to war with the ICC - and won.

> **"Kerry Packer is the man who decided to go to war with the ICC - and won."**

Gideon Haigh, the famed Aussie journalist writing for Cricinfo, described Packer as a well-known media tycoon: "...his hulking figure, heavy jaw and harsh manner making him the most recognisable businessman of his generation."

Dr. Bridget Griffen-Foley, author of *The House of Packer,* compared Kerry to his father, Sir Frank Packer: "He [Kerry Packer] was more politically opportunistic than Sir Frank and, although intensely loyal, more capable of unsentimental profiteering." The stereotypical rough won't-take-no-for-an-answer Aussie mogul, Packer, the soon-to-be billionaire, did not take the ACB's refusal kindly.

Instead, Packer - in consultation with John Cornell and Austin Robertson, two West Australian businessmen - decided that he would broadcast cricket regardless. And oh, if the ACB had said that he wasn't allowed to broadcast ACB-sanctioned cricket, what was there to stop him from creating his own league? How about a new board - one to rival the ACB? In fact - why not think even bigger? Why not challenge the ICC itself and create a new cricket empire?

These were the questions that Packer posed to himself, and answered in the affirmative. He began approaching the best cricketers in the world, both in Australia and outside, offering them massive sums of money to join his empire: the World Series Cricket.

This became the watershed moment for player pay in cricket. You must remember that even until 1975, no cricket player was a financial behemoth. Our modern-day superstars - Virat Kohli, Shahid Afridi, AB de Villiers and their ilk - have none other than Packer to thank for their magnanimous salaries. Packer, for his part, had no other option; he had to entice players to abandon the status quo of cricket and join his empire, and the only language that transcends all others is the language of money.

And, oh, boy was Packer's money convincing.

Tony Greig, the English skipper, swiftly joined Packer and - due to his high stature in the global game - promptly began "recruiting" other players to join. Clive Lloyd, the West Indies' skipper and the hero of the 1975 World Cup Final, also gave in to Packer's temptations. Imran Khan, the swashbuckling Pakistani hero and soon-to-be national captain, also agreed to Packer's demands. On the Australian side, many national heroes - Greg Chappell, Ian Chappell, Dennis Lillee, Rod Marsh - all joined Packer's World Series Cricket: a huge win for Packer in terms of garnering the attention of the Aussie audience.

In a matter of months, Packer's circus - as the impudent media initially mocked him - became a far higher quality haven of cricket than even the ICC itself could boast. Indeed, Packer's WSC Australia XI - were it to play the ICC-recognized Australian team - would have demolished their namesakes.

Packer's next task was marketing. After all, how could he make the common public get behind the WSC? How could he ensure that his stadiums filled up, while the ACB's matches remained unseen and obscure?

The answer: he launched a groundbreaking promotional campaign, popularising the now-universally-known patriotic Aussie jingle, "C'mon Aussie, C'mon!". Packer's efforts are not to be underestimated: as soon as February 1979, the song ranked No.1 on the national charts.

Nowadays, it is hard to imagine cricket without thinking about the iconic tunes associated with it. From the 2015 Cricket World Cup tune that plays in every cricket fanatic's head to this day, to the songs associated with every IPL season and PSL season - it is hard to imagine that these traditions were started by none other than a fearless entrepreneur in the 1970s.

Furthermore, this bold, brazen billionaire was (a tad oxymoronically) the first to introduce batting helmets - not for any concern for the player's well-being, oh no, but, as he remarked to Ian Chappell: "I'm not paying you to lie around in hospital for six months!"

Before you knew it, the ACB's Australian team was getting torn apart by visiting sides, while the WSC was flourishing. Gideon Haigh, writing for Cricinfo, recounts, "a game between the WSC Australians and the WSC World at the SCG in November 1978 [was] attended in excess of 50,000" - a colossal figure.

By this point, the ICC had to directly get involved.

The financial ramifications of Packer's actions were catastrophic for cricket's existing world order. The ACB's financial might had been crippled; it was on its last legs. Oh, could the ACB officials ever have predicted what was to be the outcome of their obstinacy to the Nine Network?

A key reason for Packer's success was his consumer-based approach. He was the first to conduct day-night matches: a staple of the contemporary game. Not only were these far easier for people to attend after working hours, but the cooler nightly weather, the floodlights, and the coloured uniforms all attracted larger and larger audiences.

Using drop-in pitches (another staple of today's cricketing landscape!) - a technique pioneered by Packer - prepared in greenhouses to solve logistical problems, he further cut his costs. His decision to use coloured uniforms in one-day matches, making players recognizable and instantly giving each team a unique identity, also worked wonders. Indeed, Packer's approach to monetizing cricket changed the fundamental revenue structure of cricket's core organs.

It is remarkable that the ACB could have avoided their financial catastrophe by simply giving Packer's Nine Network those broadcasting rights all those years ago! But nature has its strange ways: Packer's WSC gave cricket a much-needed boost, and its resulting popularity allows the ICC to reap the resulting financial rewards even today.

At a 1977 meeting with the ICC and ACB, Packer had made one final attempt to gain the broadcasting rights of Australian cricket matches. When the ACB continued its stubbornness, Packer stormed out with these remarkable words: "Had I got those TV rights I was prepared to withdraw from the scene and leave the running of cricket to the board. I will take no steps now to help anyone. It's every man for himself and the devil take the hindmost!"

Nonetheless, in 1979, the ACB's hand was tied: it (finally) gave in. Following the 1978-79 WSC summer, the ACB offered Packer a whopping ten-year contract that fulfilled all his financial dreams. Packer promptly called off the WSC, and cricket's rift was healed once more.

However, the aftershocks of the WSC still continue to reverberate around the world.

Packer was the first person to understand and exploit cricket's lucrative potential. Being a business bigwig and not a sportsperson, his perspective was unique. It is fair to say that the ICC could never have introduced day/night matches, coloured uniforms, drop-in pitches and the host of other innovations listed above without Packer's disruption; at the very least, the process would have been far slower.

Secondly, Packer himself had to market his product successfully to overthrow the ACB and ICC. For an entrepreneur to dethrone the established format of a century-old game is nothing short of gargantuan. To achieve this, he had to come up with the "C'mon Aussie, C'mon!" theme song, as well as schedule games at consumer-friendly hours. A competitive industry produces the best goods for the consumer, and in the ICC-WSC clash, it was the spectators and lovers of cricket that truly won.

The broadcasting industry enjoyed its boom thanks to Packer. As Gideon Haigh, writing for Cricinfo in 2010, commented: "Administrators, wakened to the value that the media imputed to their sport, came to recognise television rights as an important revenue source." The multibillion dollar broadcasting contracts we see today - fought over in high-octane bidding clashes between giants like Star Sports, SONY, and Sky - owe their origin to none other than Packer's Nine Network.

Moreover, he made the players more powerful than ever before.

England now knew that, unless they paid their cricketers handsomely, there was nothing stopping Tony Greig from joining another rebel league that paid him his dues. Similarly, Imran Khan of Pakistan and Clive Lloyd of the West Indies also understood their star power for the first time. Much like the rise of the T20 freelancer in the 21st century, Packer's league gave the players the upper-hand in contract negotiations, making them financial giants as well as sporting heroes.

"It's every man for himself and the devil take the hindmost!"
- Kerry Packer

The on-field changes to cricket cannot be discounted either. Helmets, in particular, are a tremendous legacy of Packer; although his initial plan to use yellow balls for better visibility did not see the light of day, his insight in producing coloured clothes and floodlights made cricket a far better product for all involved.

Lastly, his cultural impact shook the game. The ICC now realised it had to be on its toes: a new competitor could emerge at any time that threatened to abolish the cricketing monarchy. Indeed, since 2008, the ICC's biggest fear has been the rise of the IPL and its rapid invasion into the cricket calendar: now nearly two-and-a-half-months long and threatening to swallow the window for bilateral series entirely.

The Chinese premier, Zhou Enlai, when asked by a reporter in 1972 to comment about the influence of the 18th-century French Revolution, famously remarked: "It's too early to tell."

Similarly in 2024, it is far too early to gauge the true impact of Packer's circus.

Just how far will cricket's first experience with capitalism and the free market continue to affect it?

No singular event, perhaps, has changed cricket as much as Packer's actions did: directly catalysing a myriad of mini-revolutions in the way we view, perceive, and consume cricket. And yet, it is still too soon - especially in light of Packer-inspired T20 franchise leagues (most notably the IPL!) - to gauge its ultimate impact.

The 1992 World Cup

The only way to understand the significance of the 1992 ODI World Cup is to watch a game from 1991 and another from 1993.

The contrast is otherworldly.

On one hand, pristine whites; on the other, sponsor-littered colourful jerseys reflecting the gluttonous & glamorous modern game.

On one hand, players toiling under the sweltering sun amidst soulless stands; on the other, packed crowds cheering on their favourites in a cool nightly breeze under glaring floodlights.

On one hand, a niche sport trying to carve its place in the sporting world; on the other, a confident, booming sport with action-packed games and nail-biting thrillers.

Indeed, 1992 was the first time the ICC fully embraced its lessons from the Kerry Packer saga. The implementation of Packer's ideas - coupled with the ICC's own devices - occurred in the 1992 iteration of cricket's premier event.

For starters, the world was sent into a furore when cricket - the oh-so-typical, ever-so-classy, goody-two-shoes gentlemen's game! - decided to replace its staple white uniforms with coloured jerseys.

Furthermore, to create player marketability and increase individual stardom, player names were included on jerseys for the first time. This change showcased a new tactic which the

ICC had learnt from Packer and his marketing stunts: crafting player identities to create new (and bolster existing) rivalries - a tactic still used to this day.

> ***"The implementation of Packer's ideas - coupled with the ICC's own devices - occurred in the 1992 iteration of cricket's premier event."***

However, the ICC dared to go even further beyond what Packer had done. Rather than boost the popularity and profitability of the sport purely through marketing campaigns, the ICC made an even more groundbreaking decision: for the first time ever, they began changing the fundamental rules of the game with a view to generate more excitement.

The most revolutionary of these changes was the advent of fielding restrictions.

The ICC identified that the first hour or so of an ODI innings - with the batters still getting their eye in and the new ball swinging around corners - were dull and boring for the viewer. To rectify this, they introduced a rule that we now call the Batting Powerplay: for the first 15 overs, only two fielders could stand outside the thirty-yard circle.

This shifted the dynamics of ODI cricket. Now, the first 15 overs - rather than a dull settling period for the batsmen - was an exciting gamechanger. The batting team knew it was their best chance to score runs, so they began taking more risks. Likewise, the bowlers had the shiny new ball with them, which they could exploit unreservedly - a philosophy further aided by the provision of two new balls, one from each end, also introduced in the 1992 World Cup.

It was the astute Kiwi skipper, Martin Crowe, who first decided to exploit the new rule. Mark Greatbatch, the Kiwi opener, essentially became cricket's first "pinch-hitter": his job being simply to walk out at the start of the innings and whack every ball for the first 15 overs. England were the next team to catch on, promoting Ian Botham up the order for a similar role. It should, therefore, be no surprise to the reader that both these teams consequently topped the table in the league stage with great aplomb: a fair reward for their ingenuity.

Team	Pts	Pld	W	L	NR	T	NRR
New Zealand	14	8	7	1	0	0	0.592
England	11	8	5	2	1	0	0.470
South Africa	10	8	5	3	0	0	0.138
Pakistan	9	8	4	3	1	0	0.166
Australia	8	8	4	4	0	0	0.201
West Indies	8	8	4	4	0	0	0.076
India	5	8	2	5	1	0	0.137
Sri Lanka	5	8	2	5	1	0	-0.686
Zimbabwe	2	8	1	7	0	0	-1.142

New Zealand and England dominated the 1992 league stage, as they were the first teams to realise the importance of exploiting the newly-introduced fielding restrictions.

Sri Lanka's Sanath Jayasuriya later took Powerplay hitting to a new level in the 1996 World Cup, and ODI batting was thus drastically revolutionised forevermore. The Gayles, Bairstows, and Warners of today - the sinewy pinch-hitters and burly powerplay-exploiters - doubtless owe some of their fame to the concept of the Batting Powerplay, introduced in 1992.

Martin Crowe, the Kiwi skipper, deserves another mention here. Prior to 1992, spinners had been used exclusively for middle-overs bowling. Crowe sent shockwaves throughout the opposition camps, when, in the tournament opener against the defending champions Australia, Crowe opened the bowling with Dipak Patel, an off-spinner. Patel's economical spell - conceding just 36 in his 10 overs - negated the Batting Powerplay; Crowe went on to use the tactic with great success throughout the Cup as the Kiwis topped the league stage. To this day in limited-overs matches, spinners are used to control the economy - a strategy pioneered by Martin Crowe.

On the note of spinners, the eventual champions Pakistan also deserve a mention. Wrist-spinners were, by and large, an uncommon sight in the world of cricket - that is, until Mushtaq Ahmed took the world by storm in 1992.

Player	Team	Wkts	Mts	Ave	S/R	Econ	BBI
Wasim Akram	Pakistan	18	10	18.77	29.08	3.76	4/32
Ian Botham	England	16	10	19.12	33.3	3.43	4/31
Mushtaq Ahmed	Pakistan	16	9	19.43	29.2	3.98	3/41
Chris Harris	New Zealand	16	9	21.37	27.0	4.73	3/15
Eddo Brandes	Zimbabwe	14	8	25.35	30.0	5.05	4/21
Allan Donald	South Africa	13	9	25.30	36.0	4.21	3/34
Manoj Prabhakar	India	12	8	20.41	38.5	4.28	3/41
Anderson Cummins	West Indies	12	6	20.50	29.5	4.16	4/33
Willie Watson	New Zealand	12	8	25.08	39.5	3.81	3/37
Brian McMillan	South Africa	11	9	27.81	39.8	4.19	3/30

The leading wicket-takers of the 1992 World Cup - a list dominated by pacers, with the notable exception of Mushtaq Ahmed.

Of the top 19 wicket-takers of the 1992 World Cup, only one was a spinner - and that was Mushtaq Ahmed, enjoying himself at a joint-second place on the list. He took 16 wickets with remarkable consistency - his best figures were only 3/41! - and dominated the middle-overs in a cruel world that had hitherto paid little attention to the crafty art of wrist-spin. The wrist-spin revolution thus began: soon, Warne and Kumble would take over, and wrist-spin still acts as a focal part of world cricket, championed by Rashid Khan, Kuldeep Yadav, and Shadab Khan in the 2020s.

As the 1992 World Cup further modernised the game, the ICC also adopted the concept of sight-screens to prevent visual distractions to the bowler/batter: a much-appreciated addition, and one that displayed their dedication to improving the quality of cricket.

"For the first time ever, the ICC actively decided to alter the rules of the sport in favour of generating more excitement and entertainment."

However, cricket was still finding its feet in a consumer-based market. In its broadcast deals, the ICC made one fatal error: if the first-innings of any match had a slow over-rate, then, rather than playing out the full fifty overs, the team batting first would end its innings whenever the allotted time of the innings was completed.

Thus, Australia's games against England, South Africa, and Sri Lanka only enjoyed first innings performances of 49, 49, and 46 overs each - a blow to the side batting first, who had doubtless planned and paced their innings keeping 50 overs in mind. The iconic India vs Pakistan clash - the first time the two rivals clashed in a World Cup, another feather in the 1992 edition's cap - was also only a 49 overs vs 49 overs affair, as Pakistan's over-rate was tardy.

The matter was made even more controversial in the South Africa vs England semi-final, when the Proteas deliberately bowled slowly to end the English innings at 46 overs, denying them the chance for a death overs flourish - a logical tactic on

The most revered trophy in cricket: the Ashes urn, fought between England and Australia biennially since 1882.

In Affectionate Remembrance

OF

ENGLISH CRICKET,

WHICH DIED AT THE OVAL

ON

29th AUGUST, 1882,

Deeply lamented by a large circle of sorrowing friends and acquaintances.

R.I.P.

N.B.—The body will be cremated and the ashes taken to Australia.

The infamous Sporting Times obituary which gave birth to the "Ashes" series in 1882.

W.G. Grace - international cricket's first superstar.
Photographed by George Beldam

The Ashes: cricket's oldest rivalry.
The Cricket Monthly

Bradman had a batting average of 99.94 - by far the best in history! - prompting England to devise "Bodyline" tactics to counter his prowess.

The greatest batsman to grace the game: Sir Donald Bradman.

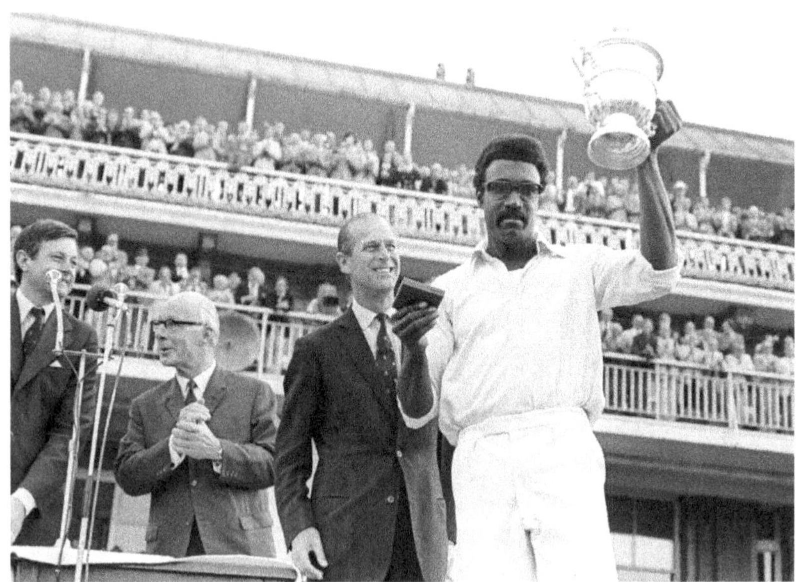

Clive Lloyd leading the West Indies to cricket's first-ever World Cup triumph: the start of a decade of dominance.

Ben Stokes' famous win at Headingley, made possible by an umpiring error with one wicket remaining! Does DRS technology need to be changed to prevent such mistakes?

Coloured jerseys, white balls, and night cricket: just a few of the revolutions catalysed by Packer's circus!

In a shocking upset, Kapil's Devils defeat the West Indies to claim the 1983 World Cup Trophy, sending India into a cricket fever that lasts to this day.

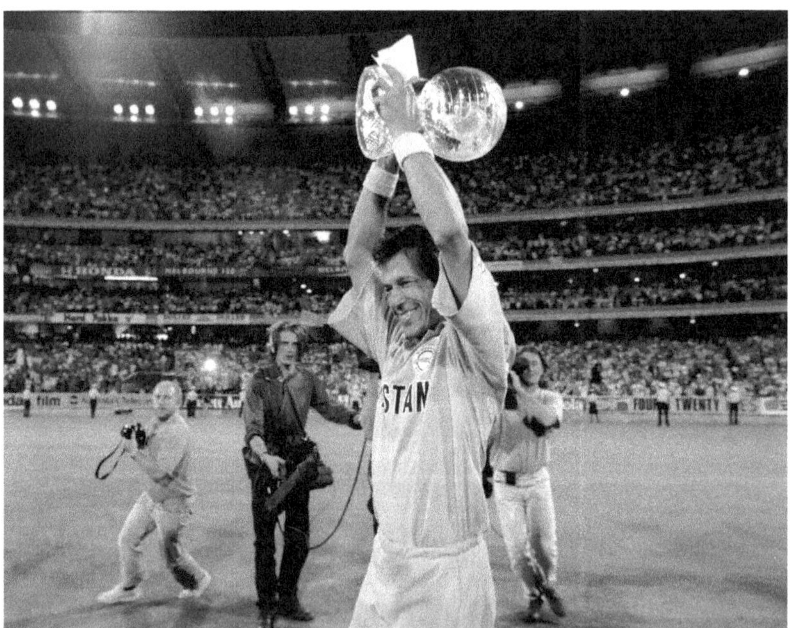

The Start of Modern Cricket: batting powerplays, fielding restrictions, and controversial rain rules finally arrive in international cricket as Imran Khan's Cornered Tigers lift the trophy!

Miandad's immortal six: a shot for the ages.

22 off 1: A rain rule fiasco costs South Africa the chance to play the 1992 World Cup Final in their first post-apartheid appearance, starting a string of "chokes" in knockout matches.

Kerry Packer and Tony Greig - the England captain playing in the World Series Cricket - conversing in 1979.

Frank Duckworth and Tony Lewis: the mathematicians who solved cricket's age-old rain crisis.

South Africa chase down 438/9 against Australia in 2006, redefining the limits of what is possible in ODI cricket.

Australia celebrating their score of 434/4, setting a new world record in ODI cricket - only for it to be broken 4 hours later!

The DRS: a flawed-yet-functioning system.

Players wait anxiously for a DRS decision to load up - a common sight in modern cricket.

The Gaylestorm: Christopher Henry Gayle smashing 175 in an IPL innings, a record that has stood the test of time.*

The Little Master: Sachin Tendulkar mastered the art of ODI batting, scoring 18,426 runs in the format.

Heinrich Klaasen belting bowlers all around the park in 2024 - the IPL's highest-ever run-scoring season. Have bowlers been reduced to mere peasants in the modern game?

The first-ever T20 match: a comical sight with Glenn McGrath recreating Trevor Chappell's infamous underarm ball!

The IPL trophy: will this ambitious franchise league usurp the international calendar?

The IPL auction, where players are bought and sold like groceries in a supermarket.

The Pakistan Super League: a cheap copy of the IPL, or the real deal?

T10 cricket: the future of the sport, or a fading fad?

NBA champions are christened the "World Champions" of their sport, despite the NBA being a national league - a blasphemous disregard for the international game. Is cricket following a similar trajectory?

The Cricket World Cup trophy: still the biggest prize in international cricket.

murky moral grounds.

In any case, the ICC sensibly rectified its broadcasting contracts for future tournaments. Such teething problems are to be expected when attempting to conduct such a revolutionary World Cup.

The format of the 1992 iteration was also remarkable: it was the first World Cup to not feature two groups, but rather have a far more equitable everyone-plays-everyone round-robin format. Although the tournament was lengthier, it simply added to the excitement as an exciting qualification race played out - not to mention the extra revenue garnered via the increased number of matches.

The tournament also produced several iconic moments that became cultural landmarks in cricket: Jonty Rhodes' flying run-out, Inzamam-ul-Haq's arrival as a superstar, Wasim Akram's back-to-back wickets in the final, and the first-ever World Cup India-Pakistan match - one that set off a string of 8 victories to India!

It is also worth answering the query of every cricket fan as to why the World Cup was held five years after the previous iteration, rather than the customary four. The answer lies in the unique climate of the southern hemisphere, where summer lasts November to March; when the Australian Cricket Board won the bid to host the 1991 iteration, they pointed out that due to the timings of their seasons, the tourney would have to be held in early 1992.

However, four years later in 1996, the World Cup was too close to the 1996 Olympics - another quadrennial event. Thus, to prevent clashes between World Cup years and Olympics years, the ICC put its tournament out of sync with the Olympics by hosting the 1999 edition only three years after its predecessor.

In any case, the 1992 World Cup altered cricket irrevocably, in a fashion that no tournament before it or after it has done. It didn't hurt that the tournament produced a new winner: Pakistan, the cornered tigers, whose daring cricket and aggressive bowling tactics were rewarded with cricket's most prestigious prize.

It is fitting that this revolutionary World Cup was held in Australia, the land of Packer, the original visionary. The changes pioneered by the 1992 World Cup - the floodlights, the coloured jerseys, the two white balls, the Powerplays, the sightscreens, the rise of wrist-spin, the innovative bowling changes, the tournament format, and many more - changed the game we love immensely - and if you ask me, all for the better!

22 *off* 1

In gully cricket, when it rains, the best solution is to call it a day and head home for supper. In a high-stakes World Cup match with glory, history, and money on the line, that typically isn't an option.

Prior to the 1992 World Cup, several methods of resolving rain-interrupted games were in use. One was a dubiously simple method to determine the revised target via the average run rate of the batting team, e.g. if the team batting first scored 200 in 50 overs at 4 runs per over, and the second innings was shortened to 30 overs due to rain, the revised par score would be 120, achieved by playing 30 overs at the same scoring rate. This system was used in the 1987 World Cup, when rain played spoilsport at the England vs Sri Lanka game.

A key flaw of this method is immediately obvious: maintaining a higher run-rate for a short number of overs is far easier than maintaining the same run-rate for a longer duration. For example, hitting 6 off 1 is far easier than hitting 36 off 6; similarly, scoring 20 off 2 overs is far easier than scoring 500 off 50, even though both are scored at the same run-rate. This flaw came to light in the 1988-89 Australian Tri-Series Final, where West Indies benefitted from the rule against hosts Australia.

Another flaw is the complete disregard for wickets lost, which can be highly impactful in second-innings interruptions. If the target is 201 in 50 overs, and the chasing team is 100/9 in 20 overs when rain falls, the chasing team would be declared the winner on the basis of their superior run-rate - an extremely unlikely outcome were the match to be played out in its totality.

Following the 1988-89 Tri-Series Final, Australian officials - no doubt chafed by the controversial defeat - set about devising a new and fairer system, seeking to mitigate the advantage provided to the chasing side in the previous system. In doing so, they effectively took an eye for an eye: rather than favouring the chasing side, they devised a Most Productive Overs formula with a heavy bias towards the defending team.

In theory, the formula would remove the least productive overs from the team batting first to calculate the revised par score. If Team A scored 250 in 50 overs, and a rain delay meant that Team B would only be able to bat for 45 overs, then the least productive 5 overs from Team A's innings would be removed from their total.

A bizarre scenario is that if Team A had faced five maiden overs, the par score would be 250 off 45 overs - essentially removing five overs from Team B's innings without any reduction in the target!

Unlike its predecessor, this system favoured the team batting first - admittedly a more equitable philosophy, as the chasing side has the benefit of knowing the target. However, once again, the system disregarded the number of wickets in hand; furthermore, it seemed to penalise the team bowling first for bowling economical overs, as evidenced by the example of the five maiden overs.

Regardless of its flaws, the system was adopted for the 1992 World Cup. Little did the rulemakers realise, this decision would result in one of the most infamous scandals in cricket history.

In Match 12, when the hosts took on India at the Gabba, Australia scored 237 off their allotted 50 overs. A fifteen-minute rain delay when India were 45/2 in 16.2 overs meant that three overs would be lost from the chasing side's innings. However, after removing Australia's three least productive overs, the target only fell by two runs - a crucial advantage for the hosts. Ironically, the game went down to the last ball, and Australia won the match by the slenderest margin of one run!

The purpose of the rain rule - to determine a fair outcome that would have likely occurred without the rain interruption - had, with a high degree of certainty, not been achieved in this match. However, this was just the beginning.

In Match 13 - played on the same day as the Australia/India nailbiter! - the would-be finalists clashed at Adelaide. Having bowled Pakistan out for 74, it seemed that a victory for England would be a mere formality. Anyone with the most rudimentary of cricketing acumen would unhesitatingly admit that chasing 75 in 300 balls would be a menial task for the English juggernaut - anyone, that is, who was unaccustomed to the rain rule.

Following a rainshower in the mid-innings break, England had 16 overs for their second innings. However, removing the least productive 34 overs of Pakistan's innings meant that the target would be 64! The required run-rate, that would have been a measly 1.50 without the rain interruption, was now 4.00 - a whopping advantage to Pakistan.

England could only muster 24/1 in their first 8 overs on a seaming cobra of a pitch, and would doubtless have slid to an unjust defeat, were it not for another rain interruption that rendered the game abandoned.

While the game is remembered for Pakistan being saved by the rain, it is little remembered that England, too, was saved from defeat by the second rain interruption. The irony is only compounded by the fact that the controversial result of this game

- with the two teams eventually sharing points - turned out to heavily influence the result of the tournament. Pakistan - who would have been knocked out had the game been played on a dry day and England chased down 75 - ended up qualifying by a whisker, and went on to win the tournament. Talk about a butterfly effect!

> **"While the game is remembered for Pakistan being saved by the rain, it is little remembered that England, too, was saved from defeat by the second rain interruption."**

Regardless, the sheer infeasibility and impracticality of the rain rule was now beyond question.

However, partially because the match was deemed as a no-result - and subsequently became less headline-worthy than if Pakistan had won after being bowled out for the lowest score in their ODI history - and partially because playing conditions cannot be changed midway through a World Cup, the rain rule stayed for the remainder of the tournament. It went on to have a crucial say in the India/Zimbabwe game, equitably giving India the advantage this time round, and then again reared its head in the almighty semi-final.

When England played the upstarts South Africa for the right to challenge Pakistan in the Final, rain was on the radar. Kepler Wessels, the Protean captain, had a tough call to make when the coin landed his way. Given that South Africa had been prolific chasers throughout the tournament, he was eager to bowl first; however, the stark advantage given to the team batting first by the rain rule encouraged him to opt to bat. Eventually, he opted to chase - a decision that would change history.

Interestingly, a non-meteorological controversy occurred in the first-innings. Due to broadcasting hurdles, three and a half hours were allotted for each innings. If, due to a slow over-rate, the quota of fifty overs could not be completed, the innings would nonetheless be ended after three and a half hours, and a monetary penalty issued to the fielding side. The crafty Proteas manipulated this rule to their advantage, bowling with a slow over rate; resultantly, the English innings culminated at 252/6 off 45 overs.

Let us pause here. This incident shows that cricket - nay, sports in general - was a stranger to capitalism at this time. While this over-rate gamesmanship can be questioned from a moral, ethical, and sporting standpoint, it is indisputable that South Africa gained an advantage from their dirty little tactic. They disoriented the batters, who would have been pacing their run-rate expecting to play 50 overs. Dermot Reeve, batting at a strike-rate of 179 when the first innings ended, could doubtless have inflicted some damage on the Protean death bowling - an opportunity he was unjustly denied.

They say history is written by the victors, but this statement seems hollow in this case. Perhaps this match was meant to be a children's fable on the inevitable failure of unethical gamesmanship, although history ended up recording it as a tragedy for the valiant South Africans! Perhaps, the calamity that followed was cricket's revenge at the Proteas' infidelity.

After a twisting and turning game, the Saffers needed 22 off the last 13. No Protean scored a fifty, but through a thorough team effort, they managed to amass 231/6 off 42.5 overs. McMillan and Richardson were at the crease, and the packed Sydney crowd anticipated a roaring climax: who would fall - the two-time finalists or the rising upstarts?

To their dismay, nothing fell but water from the heavens. Two overs were resultantly lost.

As South Africa had bowled two maiden overs - conceding a leg-bye in one of them - the revised target would be decreased from 253 to 252, at the expense of two overs. As a result, the Proteas would require 21 off 1 ball.

The giant screen initially displayed: "South Africa to win: need 22 runs off 7 balls", which was then amended to the infamous image we all know: 22 off 1. Ironically, neither was the correct equation - the officials had neglected the leg-bye - but what difference did it make?

What difference did it make to the enraged McMillan, who jogged a meaningless single and jostled off the pitch? What difference did it make to the sheepish-but-jubilant Englishmen, who became three-time finalists - and promptly, three-time runners-ups? What difference did it make to the world of cricket, except that a shocking farce was played out that resonates with our emotions to this very day?

Yet another irony that is often neglected - the match had been allocated a Reserve Day which could have been used to prevent the controversy. However, the ICC only allows a game to go into a Reserve Day if every effort to conclude the game on the same day fails.

I vehemently disagree with this policy, and cite the 1992 semi-final as a case study. Firstly, the broadcasting rules should never have been so strict to force England's innings to be concluded five overs too early (a policy which the ICC eventually rectified). Secondly, after the cessation of the downpour at 22 off 13, every effort should have been made to play out the full 2.1 overs under the floodlights. Thirdly, if that was not possible, I am sure both teams and the crowd would have been happier to play out 22 off 13 on the Reserve Day rather than watch McMillan knock a single with 21 needed off 1. To this day, the ICC remains stubborn about its suboptimal use of the Reserve Day.

Say that an ODI is due to be played on 1st August with 2nd

August as its Reserve Day. If rain falls on the morning of the first day until four hours of play remain, then the ICC would rather that the teams play a 20-over game to decide the winner on the 1st itself, rather than play out the full 50 overs for both sides by utilising the Reserve Day as well. This, in my opinion, is a criminal underutilisation of the concept of the Reserve Day, and I fear a looming controversy that will eventually force the ICC to amend its policy.

"To this day, the ICC remains stubborn about its suboptimal use of the Reserve Day."

Another consequence of the "22 off 1 game" was the introduction of the D/L system to resolve rain-marred matches. Following the 1992 fiasco, the ICC sought alternative solutions, ratifying a more complex mathematical system at its July 1995 meeting, whereby the target score would be determined by multiplying the score of the team batting first by a percentage factor. The system was arguably better than its predecessors - admittedly a very low bar.

In the meantime, two British statisticians - Frank Duckworth and Tony Lewis - set about devising a mathematical formula to provide reasonable, fair, and objective resolutions for interrupted cricket limited-overs matches. It is remarkable that their achievements are mathematical, not sporting, yet cricket fans are more accustomed to their names than those of many a talented player.

The Duckworth/Lewis method, as their formula was christened, sought to resolve cricket's age-old crisis of dealing with rain interruptions. The secret of the formula's success is its philosophy to think about a cricketing innings in terms of its remaining "resources", i.e. overs and wickets. Using these two data points, it uses an exponential decay function to calculate suitable par scores depending on the match situation. While the exact values of the parameters used in the mathematical formula are not made publicly available, they are based on values from "hundreds of one-day internationals", in the statisticians' own words.

The D/L method (short for Duckworth/Lewis) was first used in 1997; it was officially adopted by the ICC in 1999, and remains cricket's rain guru. However, the formula has not been without amendments.

In the early 2000s, Tony Lewis and Frank Duckworth realised that the game of cricket was rapidly evolving. When Australia smashed 359 in the 2003 World Cup Final, its inventors began to see the formula's inability to deal with large totals. To rectify this, the formula was updated in 2004; this new version became known as the Professional Edition and was promptly incorporated into the ICC Playing Handbook, whereas the previous formula was named the Standard Edition.

In 2009, the formula was again updated to adjust to the new T20 format. When the pioneers of the formula, Professors Duckworth and Professor Lewis retired in late 2014, the custodianship of the formula was handed to Professor Steven Stern of Australia.

The method was promptly renamed to the Duckworth/Lewis/ Stern method, or DLS for short.

However, these three were not the only mathematicians who sought to appease cricket followers.

In 2002, an Indian engineer, V. Jayadevan, presented his new rain rule for cricket. Christened the VJD method, the formula largely performs similarly to the DLS system, albeit with one key difference: VJD assumes an ODI innings to score fast during the Powerplay, decelerate in the middle overs, and accelerate at the death; DLS, by contrast, assumes a typical ODI innings to accelerate throughout, with the acceleration being more rapid at the end than at the start.

The VJD method has been used primarily in the Indian cricketing circuit, including the Tamil Nadu Premier League and Vijay Hazare Trophy. Professor Jayadevan and Professor Stern have both written articles on ESPN Cricinfo critiquing one another's methods and illuminating the cricket world as to the inner workings of both formulae.

Frankly, I'm happy with either of these methods as long as we stay clear from the Most Productive Overs abomination!

It is worth noting that the 1992 semi-final set off a string of close-but-no-cigar moments for South Africa in ICC events. After the heartbreaking rain-marred fiasco against England in 1992, they were in a commanding position in the 1996 quarter-final at 186/3 chasing 265 against the West Indies, before a late collapse dashed their hopes. In 1999, they tied the semi-final against Australia - considered by many to be the greatest ODI ever played - when Allan Donald froze in his tracks and ran himself out in the final over, as they failed to advance on the basis of net-run-rate. In 2003, the rain rule once again returned to haunt them, as they misunderstood the D/L par score and ended up tying the match rather than winning it, failing to qualify. In 2007, their old foes, the Aussies, returned to thrash them in the semi-final en route to their third successive trophy. In 2009, they succumbed to eventual-champions Pakistan in the semi-final by seven runs, failing to close out the game at the death. In 2011, the Proteas were in a comfortable position at 108/2 chasing 222 against the Kiwis, before a middle-order collapse brought their campaign to a screeching halt. In 2015, in another rain-affected game (how dearly would the Proteas have hated precipitation by now!), a South-Africa-born player playing for the Black Caps dealt a killing blow to their dreams as he smashed a six with 5 needed off 2 balls in a last-over nailbiter. In 2023, they played out a humdinger against eventual-champions Australia, losing by three wickets, as Australia chased down the very target the Proteas had been bowled out for in 1999, rubbing salt in the old wound. When, at long last, they got past the semi-final hurdle in the T20 World Cup 2024, India prevailed over them by the slender margin of 7 runs to deny them their maiden World Cup triumph.

Oh, South Africa! Ever so valiant, yet ever so nervy!

How different could things have been, had McMillan and Richardson stolen 22 runs from those precious 13 deliveries? How might they have crushed the same Pakistani side whom they had already hammered in the league stage? And oh, riding on the confidence of their maiden World Cup victory, how differently might all those near-misses have turned out?

Alas, we will never know.

The Impossible Chase

The year is 2006.

Australia, the dominant team of the day, have broken yet another record - a regular habit for them in the 2000s. This time, they had produced the highest total in ODI history, clobbering South Africa for 434.

To add insult to injury, they had pounded the Proteas at their own den in Johannesburg; to further compound their misery, they had reserved this performance for the series-decider. A closely-fought series, tied at 2-2, was all but over as the vanquished Proteas traipsed off the field.

What followed, however, is something the likes of which have neither been seen before or since.

South Africa, rather than meekly accepting defeat, took on the challenge of chasing 435. First came Smith and Gibbs, then later came Boucher and van der Wath, but the barrage of boundaries never stopped. Despite regular wickets and a Nathan Bracken fifer, South Africa's intent never faltered, until they needed 1 to win, and Boucher chipped it down the ground for four.

The task was achieved; the mission was complete; and the impossible chase had been overcome.

It is interesting to note that, despite batting becoming easier as time went on, 438/9 in 49.5 remains the highest chase in ODI history - in fact, in international cricket history. It is equally interesting to reflect that this game could never have occurred in the 1980s or 1990s: an era when chasing 235 - let alone 435! - was headline-worthy news.

Today, the ICC believes that the best way to market cricket is through sixes and fours. A six, they argue, is universal: even a baseball fan can recognize that when the ball goes all the way, it's a "home run". The concept of wickets, however, hardly exists in any other sport.

Take the example of the IPL - a competition with the sole purpose of maximising the BCCI's profit. Unlike the ICC, the IPL bears no responsibility to "preserve the balance between bat and ball" or act as "custodians of the game". Rather, they simply do whatever it takes to make their brand more lucrative - and in 2024, the floodgates were opened for the bat to dominate the ball.

The 2024 edition saw batting records tumble: a new highest score, a new highest successful chase, a new highest powerplay score, a new record for most sixes per match, and dozens more! Eight of the nine highest scores in IPL history were scored in this edition; five of the six highest second-innings scores were also seen in 2024. Somewhere, somehow, for some reason, the organisers of the tournament decided to obliterate the hearts of bowlers around the globe.

The tournament saw an average scoring rate of 9.56 r.p.o, the highest in its history by a massive margin of 0.57 r.p.o - more than half a run every over: a staggering difference.

But the million-dollar question is: why?

Are modern-day batsmen just that good? Surely not; it seems unlikely that an ageing Sunil Narine - a bowler for heaven's sake! - has scored a T20 century in the supposedly highest-quality league in the world!

Are the pitches just that flat? A fair question, and probably one that needs to be answered in the affirmative. Indeed, the shocking lack of any cracks or grass on most IPL pitches - a move designed to curb the bowlers' weapons of seam, turn, and variable bounce - has aided batsmen immensely.

Are the boundaries smaller? An interesting question. Cricket has always been a unique sport in that its field size has never been fixed: you always know exactly how long a football field is or how long a tennis court is, but the size of a cricket boundary can - according to Law 19.1.3 - vary from 59 metres to 82 metres - quite a massive difference! Should the ICC, then, introduce some more uniformity in boundary size - perhaps fix it at 70 metres for all grounds?

"The 2024 IPL season saw an average scoring rate of 9.56 r.p.o, the highest in the tournament's history by a massive margin of 0.57 r.p.o - more than half a run every over: a staggering difference."

Are the bats too good? Again, a fair query, and again, one that must be answered in the affirmative. Virat Kohli is an excellent player, don't get me wrong - but were he to be provided with Don Bradman's willow from a century ago, he would more likely think of it as a gardening tool than something to smack bowlers with.

If anything, to uphold justice, the ICC should strive to improve the ball just like modern bats have been improved. Surely Dukes or Kookaburra can design a ball whose seam and swing last twenty overs? Yet, bizarrely - the ICC, too, seem to wish success upon batsmen and death upon bowlers: over the years, every ball produced seems to provide less and less movement.

Are the bowlers, then, not good enough? Again, unlikely: in the far more challenging Test format, where the red cherry swings and seams and zips and turns and jags away from the batsmen in a way the white ball can only dream of doing, the batting averages are at an all-time low. No; the bowlers' skill doesn't seem to be the issue.

To illustrate the point further - the bowlers have, if anything, improved massively over the years. The slower ball, the yorker, and the knuckleball - borrowed from baseball and popularised by Zaheer Khan in the early 2010s - are now key additions to a white-ball bowler's arsenal. The slower bouncer, the double-bluff, and the wide yorker are also balls that any 1990s bowler would never have dreamt of bowling, yet which today's death-bowling specialists nail with robotic consistency. No; the bowlers' arsenal - especially in white-ball cricket - seems to be more powerful than ever.

Is the problem, then, with the fielding restrictions? Potentially, yes: the ODI batting Powerplay, as well as the first six overs of T20s, are now seeing higher scores than ever before. But, bizarrely, the imagination harks back to the 1990s, when the Powerplay lasted for 15 overs: if fielding restrictions were really the reason for the batters' dominance, why, then, did we not see even larger scores back then?

> **"Virat Kohli is an excellent player, don't get me wrong - but were he to be provided with Don Bradman's willow from a century ago, he would more likely think of it as a gardening tool than something to smack bowlers with!"**

Why, then, is the question - why the change in batting scores?

Who decided to treat bowlers with such disdain? Who decided that T20s should not be 150-par matches, but 250-par slugfests? Who decided that the batters should rule the cricketing world, while the bowlers are left to survive on the crumbs?

The answer: the batsmen themselves.

Sure, each of the above factors are contributors in their own way - smaller boundaries, flatter surfaces, stronger bats - but the biggest revolution in modern-day cricket occurred not on the cricket field, but rather, within the batsmen's mind.

Think about the three-point revolution in the NBA: although a three-pointer is a riskier shot to try, statisticians realised that the average payoff from an attempted three-pointer was higher than that of a two-pointer. Similarly, with the rise of data analytics, a new discovery was made in cricket: batters weren't attacking enough.

This realisation was most revolutionary in T20 cricket, where batsmen are free to take more risks - after all, getting bowled out in 120 balls is a rarity, so why not go big or go home?

Gradually, batsmen began adopting harder-hitting strategies. Chris Gayle, the original T20 maestro, realised the principle of boundaries: whichever team hit more boundaries is massively more likely to win a game of cricket - in both ODIs and T20s. And thus, a typical Gayle over soon became 0, 0, 4, 0, 6, 4 - the bowler could be happy with his three dots, and Gayle would gleefully romp home with a strike rate of over 200!

When you only have 120 balls, singles and dots are a victory for the bowler.

Sure, the 2024 IPL had massive scores, but let us consider: according to Cricinfo, batsmen scored 62.7% of their runs in boundaries this year - a record-breaking change in batting mentality and aggression. Is it, then, a surprise that so many records tumbled?

Additionally, the tournament had an average rate of 40.09%

balls attacked - by far the highest in its history. Is it, then, a surprise that the list of the IPL's highest scores was revamped and rewritten?

As for the champions, the Kolkata Knight Riders, they attacked a staggering 45.45% of balls faced - is it, then, a surprise that they won?

Moreover, look at the case of Jake Fraser-McGurk - the young Aussie bursting onto the scene. In a mid-IPL analysis, Sidharth Monga declared on Cricinfo that Fraser-McGurk had attacked 77 out of the 104 balls he faced - and boy did he reap the rewards!

Credit for this change in philosophy is owed - in no small measure - to the data revolution in cricket. When England, after a dismal 2015 ODI World Cup campaign, decided to adopt a data-driven approach under Eoin Morgan's leadership, they became the world's most aggressive, daring, and fastest-scoring team. Fittingly in 2019, they won the World Cup on boundary countback: perhaps the universe's way of showing us that their increased aggressiveness and boundary-driven approach was the key to their success. They followed it up in 2022 by adding the T20 World Cup to their collection - the first-ever team to hold both white-ball trophies simultaneously.

England, interestingly, took their aggressive approach even into Test cricket: thus was Bazball formed under Ben Stokes' captaincy and Brendon McCullum's strategizing. Before their partnership, the English team was stuck in a red ball rut; since then, they have played eight Test series, losing only one: a startling shift in fortunes.

Coming back to the 438 game, I ask you one simple question: if South Africa were not chasing 435, could they ever have gotten such a high score?

If South Africa were normally batting against Australia, say in a typical first innings at Johannesburg, they would probably aim for 275 as a par score. If they felt the wicket was flat, they might make a go for 320, but no more.

However, when they were given a target of 435 - they achieved it with a ball to spare.

When they realised they had no option but to attack every ball, take risks, and hit boundaries, they found to their own surprise that this strategy worked best.

And yet, from the next game onwards, they never tried to repeat the feat!

Think about it - every batsman is selfish. Every batsman tries to play themselves in, preserve their wicket, and hit boundaries whenever they get a loose ball. Gradually, though, a more aggressive mindset is settling into the players' heads: the optimal cricketing strategy in T20 and ODI matches is, quite simply, to go berserk.

Think about Australia's 434/4: surely, at the innings break, they would have felt themselves to be invincible! Yet it must be observed that they did not fully utilise their batting resources. Why, if they had taken more risks and ended up at 450/9, they would almost certainly have won the match!

Look at Pakistan in the 2023 ODI World Cup, a team known for scoring slowly and depending upon its top-order anchors - yet, when push came to shove and they had to chase down 402 against the Kiwis to stay in contention, they managed to do it (albeit with DLS assistance)!

This, in fact, is the whole reason why chasing is so advantageous in limited-overs cricket. It allows you to pace yourself and take risks accordingly. However, if teams only adopted a more daring approach, the first-innings can be just as fruitful.

> ***"Why, if Australia had taken more risks and ended up at 450/9 rather than 434/4, they would almost certainly have won the match!"***

Jacques Kallis, in the mid-innings break in Johannesburg, saw the despairing faces of his compatriots. Ever an optimist, Kallis joked: "Bowlers, we've done a great job and Australia are 15 runs short!"

His dry humour got a few laughs; the batters then began plotting how to chase down the target.

Little did he know how true his words rang.

The Boulder of Sisyphus

"Here we go. The crowd cheers - here's Siddle! Oh, that ball was close! He's given it! He's given him! Peter Siddle's got a hat-trick on his birthday! You beauty!"

"Not yet he hasn't," interrupts Mark Nicholas dryly, killing the fun like a school bell declaring recess to be finished. "Not yet he hasn't, because England will challenge that. Settle down, boys."

The Australians pause their celebrations. The crowd quietens while the third umpire boots up the ball-tracking software. Stuart Broad stands lamely in the middle of the pitch, not sure where to go - his confused expression uncannily resembling one whose birthday song is being sung, and they don't know whether to join in or stay quiet!

Eventually - one-and-a-half minute after Aleem Dar raised his finger - he raises it again, noticeably less firmly this time. The Australians regroup to celebrate Siddle's achievement, and the crowd cheers again, albeit several decibels lower this time.

The jarring image described above - of how an iconic Ashes moment was diminished by the interruption of technology - is one that every cricketing fan can relate to. However, for more than a century, the word of the umpire was sacred, incontrovertible, and utterly final. The maxim that every budding cricketer is universally taught - "Respect the umpire's call, sonny!" - was questioned for the first time.

DRS - the Decision Review System - challenged the sacredness of the umpire's call, and the world of cricket is still reeling from the seismic effects of the decision to revoke the finality of the umpire's decision. The non-uniformity of the application of DRS, the subjectivity that still exists within the software, and the disruption to the flow of the game - as seen in the case of Siddle's Ashes hat-trick - has continuously provoked observers to critique the system's implementation.

The ICC's quest to reach objectivity in umpiring decisions bears similarity to the Greek mythological figure Sisyphus: as a punishment for his crimes, Sisyphus was condemned to roll a boulder up a steep hill endlessly in the Underworld, for eternity. Much like the fruitlessness of Sisyphus's efforts, the goal to make umpiring decisions in cricket fully objective is also, inevitably, futile.

Our story, however, begins not in Ancient Greece, but in Pakistan in 1986.

In an age where all Tests and ODIs were adjudicated by local umpires (due to the mere logistical ease of the matter), it is indisputable that bias in decision-making was rampant. The case of Javed Miandad, the swashbuckling Pakistani run-machine, is an oft-quoted example: at home, he was only dismissed LBW 8 times in 76 dismissals, significantly lower than his career tally of 33 LBWs in 168 dismissals. In the land of his arch-rivals, India, though, he was dismissed LBW a staggering 8 times in only 19 innings - a suspiciously frequent occurrence.

The ugly truth is that this treatment was not unique to Miandad. Indeed, players all over the world moaned about umpiring decisions after every away defeat.

The ICC - true to its character - proceeded to do absolutely nothing to solve the problem. Zero. Zip. Zilch. Nada.

The inaction of the ICC has been a theme in several chapters in this book - from the alienation of North American and Latin American cricket in the early 1900s, to the delay in adopting ODIs as an international format, to the procrastination in establishing a World Cup - the list goes on and on. I need not waste the reader's time by further lambasting the governing organisation's trademark tardiness.

"At home, Javed Miandad was dismissed LBW only 8 times in 76 dismissals - significantly lower than his career tally of 33 LBWs in 168 dismissals."

In any case, Imran Khan, the dashing Pakistani skipper, decided to put an end to the constant bickering that followed every home series. Prior to the 1986 Pakistan vs West Indies Test series - the premier rivalry of world cricket in the 80s - Khan invited two Indian umpires to officiate the matches, and the move was well-received. He later invited two English umpires to officiate the Pakistan v India series in 1989-90, and the ICC eventually caught on: in 1992, one neutral umpire per Test was declared mandatory, and ten years later, both field umpires were required to be neutral.

History regards this change as a wholly positive one: umpiring howlers went down, impartiality increased, and the gentleman's game became a fairer sport. However, all hell broke loose in 2008 at Sydney.

A close-fought Border-Gavaskar Test, in the dying hours of Day 5, ended in favour of the Aussies; however, the high quality of cricket that had been played by both teams across the game was overshadowed by controversy.

The Indian eleven - already disillusioned with the "Monkeygate" sledging saga - felt they had been hard done by several umpiring decisions by Steve Bucknor and Mark Benson, which had ultimately cost them the game. As the furore rose to a crescendo, the ICC had to put its foot down - and for the first time in cricketing history, the fundamental status of the umpire's decision was called into question.

The 2000s were undoubtedly a decade of immense technological advancement: the rise of the internet, the invention of the smartphone, and the launch of social media, all irreversibly changed the world at the dawn of the new millennium - for better or for worse. And soon, in a small niche at the confluence of sports and technology, seismic shifts began to occur.

Tennis was the first to take advantage: contracting a sports technology company to use the Hawk-Eye ball-tracking software, tennis began monitoring close line calls via technology. In tennis, however, the matter was binary: the ball is either in or out. In cricket, on the other hand, the matter is far murkier.

For example, in an LBW decision, the Hawk-Eye system is not merely observing whether the ball bounced before a particular point or not (as is the case in tennis). Rather, the system used in cricket is predictive: it has to determine whether or not the ball would have gone on to hit the stumps or not. This fundamentally changes the nature of the technology required: the software must be predictive rather than merely detectional.

> *"The 2000s were a decade of immense technological advancement: the rise of the internet, the invention of the smartphone, and the launch of social media, all irreversibly changed the world at the dawn of the new millennium."*

Secondly, cricket has far more variables involved. A human operator has to judge the point of pitching and the point of impact, and whether or not they are in-line with the wicket; after this, the predictive software has to determine whether the ball was too high, too wide, or hitting the wicket. Oh, and before all of this, a separate analysis needs to be done on whether the batsman edged the ball or not! In some cases, there are even more variables that need to be considered, e.g. whether a shot was attempted or not - a complicated broth of many ingredients!

The LBW concept in cricket is unlike any other concept in any other sport; Hawk-Eye may have had its easy money in tennis, but cricket was a far harder nut to crack. As the cricket historian Gerald Brodribb famously remarked in 1995: "No dismissal has produced so much argument as LBW; it has caused trouble from its earliest days." Little did he know how hard his statement would hit home, even in 2008!

Nonetheless, the necessary software was developed, and DRS - the Decision Review System - was trialled by the ICC in 2008 and 2009, and soon became a staple of the modern game. Its implementation is well-known to every cricket follower: close calls are adjudicated according to the decision of the umpire, and players have a limited number of reviews per innings. Despite initial resistance from the BCCI - citing reservations about the accuracy of the predictive software - the system swiftly became accepted within the cricketing fraternity.

"No dismissal has produced so much argument as LBW; it has caused trouble from its earliest days."

Let us now reflect on the ramifications of the introduction of DRS.

Firstly, it irrevocably diminished the lofty status umpires once enjoyed. From the supreme judges of the cricket field, they now became mere advisors to the technology. As vindicated players thumped their chests with adrenaline after every successful review, the umpires bashfully reversed their call in embarrassment - a stark contrast from a bygone era.

Although cricket has largely remained safe from the scandals of frustrated players ranting at referees - unfortunately a common sight in football and tennis! - purists fear that with the advent of DRS, such sights will soon be prevalent on the cricket pitch. In any case, it should be noted that umpires still have far more say in cricket than in most other sports: it is they who analyse the HotSpot or Ultra-Edge data to determine a caught-behind dismissal, it is they who examine dubious catches frame-by-frame to ascertain the batsman's fate, and it is they whose decision stands when the Hawk-Eye technology is rendered inconclusive. At any rate, we are still far from the day when the umpire is a mere scarecrow.

Secondly, it added a new tactical element to the game. Previously, a denied appeal was forgotten about; now, following every rejected appeal, the bowler and batsman - often with the wicket-keeper, whose importance has vastly increased thanks to DRS due to his ideal vantage point - engage in a hurried discussion to see whether the decision should be reviewed. Every appeal now has three possible results: out, not-out, and "worth a try, skip?"

Moreover, the technology has also fundamentally altered how cricket is played: Sambit Bal of Cricinfo, analysing the impact of DRS on the modern game in 2018, writes: "Leg-before dismissals for spinners have risen by nearly 17% after the DRS came into effect. And the number of LBW dismissals to spin per Test in the ten-year period before DRS, which was 1.69, has increased to 2.56 in the last five years." The realisation across the cricketing world that umpires had massively underestimated how likely spinners were to hit the wicket - a sentiment corrected by the DRS - caused the spinners' boom to occur across all formats in the 2010s.

The DRS, however, is not without its flaws.

At Headingley in 2019, a nail-biting Test ended in favour of England after a last-wicket partnership carried them to victory; however, at 357-9 chasing 359, Ben Stokes ought to have been declared out LBW, but an umpiring gaffe allowed him to survive. Although Hawk-Eye showed the batsman to be out, the Australians had already wasted all their reviews, so Stokes could not be declared out, and he subsequently hit the winning runs for England.

This incident is a prime example of the problem with DRS and its implementation. If the technology was instantly able to show that Ben Stokes should have been out, why should it matter whether the Australians have enough "reviews" left or not? Why should the umpire not be able to refer the decision instantly to the third umpire and let technology provide a clear answer? England need 2 runs to win with one and a half day left to play: surely the players can wait thirty seconds for Hawk-Eye to load? The commonly-cited excuse that reviewing every decision would take too much time is utterly nonsensical when the chasing team merely requires a single good shot from nine possible hours of play remaining: surely the ICC should adjust the rules to allow all decisions to be reviewed when time is no longer a limiting factor!

This brings me to my central point: I fundamentally disagree with the way the ICC utilises the DRS technology. As a trial basis in 2008-09, the player referral system was workable; however, a long-term solution to improve umpiring decisions could only have been achieved by placing DRS at the disposal of the umpires. If an umpire is unsure about a particular decision - say, a close call at the fag end of a Test match, a la Headingley - let him refer it to the third umpire! Let justice prevail - regardless of how many decisions have been reviewed previously!

Fundamentally, the players should not be in control of DRS.

Let them focus on their gameplay, and let the umpires handle the decision-making. Nor do players use reviews entirely responsibly: in the 2020 England vs West Indies Test series, the latter used DRS reviews merely as a time-wasting tactic as well, reviewing random balls to hasten England's declaration. Such a fiasco would never occur if the technology was simply used optimally: allow the umpires to refer close calls whenever they feel in doubt, and let plumb LBWs be called out and done with!

Critics would level the objection that this might lead to time delays if too many decisions are reviewed.

Firstly, I disagree - I believe that the ICC's elite panel of qualified umpires are capable of making the majority of decisions without needing technological aid, and only fringe cases - one or two dismissals per innings - will need to be reviewed.

Secondly, so what if the process takes time? Does not a Test match last five days? Are the forty to fifty seconds used in upholding the game's justice not a worthy use of time for a sport that already takes up a week? If the players are giving their heart and soul on the field, the very least that the officials owe them are correct umpiring calls - especially so, when the technology to verify those calls is already present!

Ian Chappell, writing for Cricinfo, argues in a similar vein: "Surely it's time to put any review system in the hands of the umpires so that it stops being a tactic, rids the game of the howler, and on most occasions, brings a satisfactory outcome."

"Are the forty to fifty seconds used in upholding the game's justice not a worthy use of time for a sport that already takes up a week?"

Moreover, LBWs are not the only aspect of decision-making in cricket. In fact, let us hark back to one of the most recent scandals in cricket umpiring.

At the biggest stage in world cricket, England and New Zealand battled it out at Lord's for the World Cup trophy in 2019. With 9 needed off 3, Stokes attempted a risky double after striking the ball to deep midwicket.

The fielder - Guptill - fired a swift throw to the keeper, only for the ball to be intercepted by the willow of the diving batsman. The deflected ball sped away to the boundary, as the umpire - Kumar Dharmasena - awarded six runs to England for the quote-unquote "overthrow": two runs that the batsmen ran, and four runs for the boundary - a dream result for England. As a bonus, Stokes kept the strike for the next delivery as well.

The match - as I'm sure you know! - ended in a tie, and the subsequent Super Over also ended in a tie, with the trophy going to England on boundary countback, a rule that no longer exists.

However, the controversy surrounds ball 49.4. Simon Taufel, a five-time winner of the ICC's Umpire of the Year award, announced to the cricketing world that England should only have been awarded five runs for the overthrow, based on Law 19.8. Analysis from ESPN Cricinfo's Andrew Miller further supported the umpire's view. Indeed, the misjudgement of the on-field umpires to give England an extra undeserved run quite possibly tilted the fate of that epic final in 2019! What's more, according to the correct interpretation of the rules, not only should England have been awarded one run less, but Ben Stokes should have been at the non-striker's end, while his compatriot Adil Rashid should have faced the incoming delivery - a far less competent batter!

"Indeed, the misjudgement of the on-field umpires to give England an extra undeserved run quite possibly tilted the fate of that epic final in 2019!"

There are several things to discuss here.

Firstly, yes, you may say that the umpires are human after all, and such mistakes can happen in chaotic moments with tremendous pressure on not only the players, but match officials as well. What's more, overthrows aren't exactly a daily occurrence in cricket - especially not bat-deflected overthrows that go to the boundary with a World Cup trophy on the line!

However, a spade must be called a spade.

The three umpires officiating cricket's largest spectacle are the best the ICC has to offer. It is their job to know the rulebook inside out; indeed, if a retired Taufel sitting on his armchair at home can work out that England should have only gotten five runs, then why can't the world's supposedly-best umpires do the same with all the camera angles available to them at Lord's? When Imran Khan fought for umpiring fairness in 1986, he surely would not have intended to witness such a fiasco in 2019!

You may argue that the umpires had too little time on their hands to arrive at the correct conclusion. This, however, is not an opinion I can tolerate.

In tennis, a single game can go on for as long as it takes to determine a fair winner. Federer and Nadal fighting in the dying light of a Wimbledon evening in 2008 remains an iconic moment of the sport to this day, as does the Isner-Mahut game of 2010 that lasted for three days! When a sport's biggest prizes are being dished out, there is no place for hastiness - let the umpires take as much time as they need to ensure that justice is served, especially in a game where even the tiebreaker was eventually tied!

Here lies another objection of mine to the current system of DRS: if it is obvious that a game will end with ample time remaining (e.g. Headingley 2019), or if a game possesses tremendous importance (e.g. a World Cup final or an Ashes decider), the limit on the number of reviews must be removed. This holds particularly true for matches with reserve days (including all ICC finals!) where time should never be a concern in the first place! And if logistics or time are a concern, then use the floodlights or employ a Reserve Day - in short, take a leaf out of tennis's book and ensure the correct result is reached at! The ICC's utilisation of reserve days is also suboptimal, as discussed in Chapter Five.

Moreover, on the topic of DRS reviews, it is worth noting a glaring loophole in the cricketing rulebook: if a batsman is declared out by LBW, the ball is immediately declared dead, even if a DRS review later shows it to be not-out.

How is this, then, a loophole? Take the example of the 2019 IPL Final: with 2 needed off 1, Lasith Malinga trapped Shardul Thakur LBW to seal the trophy for the Mumbai Indians. Thakur promptly reviewed the umpire's decision, but to no avail.

Now, imagine that Thakur's review had been successful and he ran a leg-bye in the meantime. Logically, as his review was successful, his leg-bye should be counted and the game declared a tie!

However, here lies the catch: the game would still be awarded to the bowling team, because as soon as the on-field umpire raised his finger, the ball was immediately considered dead and no more leg-byes would be counted. What an unjust rule for the batter, and woe to cricket if this loophole comes back to bite it in the future!

In any case, it is the ICC's duty to review - and patch - these loopholes before it is too late, a la the boundary countback rule. Certainly, cricket still has a long way to go before becoming a fully just sport.

After all, achieving 100% objectivity in any umpiring decision - least of all a predictive affair, which LBWs inherently are - is as possible as Sisyphus pushing his boulder to the summit. Nonetheless, it is the duty of the custodians of the game to use the existing technology to make decision-making as accurate and transparent as possible - even if Sisyphus cannot succeed, does he not continue to persevere endlessly for his mission?

The Rise of T20

On December 12th, 2021, Lewis Hamilton was driving serenely at the Abu Dhabi Grand Prix, effortlessly dominating the race and looking set to break Michael Schumacher's iconic record of seven Formula 1 World Championships.

As the chequered flag got nearer, the crowd stood up, cheering on the legend for one final triumph. Hamilton's team looked calm and relaxed, enjoying that rare moment of trepidation that accompanies the sensation of conquering a summit hitherto unbreached by humanity. A fitting finale, a hero's hurrah, a fairytale finish: it all seemed to be going perfectly.

That is, until the Race Director, Michael Masi, threw the rulebook out of the window.

Following a crash with six laps to go, Masi chose to unlap only the cars between Hamilton and his title-rival Max Verstappen - gifting an unfair advantage to the latter. Although the race was expected to end without any more green-flag racing, Masi artificially superseded the rulebook and called in the Safety Car one lap earlier than expected - thus allowing Verstappen the chance to pass Hamilton and win the championship.

Had the rules been followed, Hamilton would have won the championship in a boring, one-sided race for the fifth consecutive year of his domination. Instead, Masi, by disregarding the rules of racing, was able to manufacture a thrilling last-lap winner-takes-all showdown that drew the attention of fans all over the globe and allowed a new face to inherit his first championship.

In a world where cricket teeters on the precipice between preserving the ardent meritocracy of Tests and milking the glitzy T20 cash-cow, the example of Formula 1 is a dangerous one: sure, entertainment and excitement has its place, but just how far is too far?

Sport is entertainment, first and foremost. Ancient cave paintings and historical relics depict humans playing rudimentary forms of modern-day sports - including sprinting and wrestling - from well over 15,000 years ago. The enjoyment, entertainment, and excitement derived from sport is an undeniable, intrinsic, and innate ingredient of the human condition.

However, while excitement and joy may be the ultimate objective of sporting endeavours, there is far more to most games than mere entertainment. Without a set of rules to govern play, any game would descend into chaos. Without merit, justice, and fairness, a win would be devoid of any meaning. Good play must always be rewarded, and bad execution penalised: any sport that fails to do this is actually just a display of luck and chance rather than skill and strategy.

Cricket's five-day red-ball format has always been a shining beacon of justice. Upsets were rare, and many sessions went by where the most exciting thing was nothing but a rejected appeal for caught-behind, but the best team almost always won after five days!

> ***"Sure, entertainment and excitement has its place, but just how far is too far?"***

By the 2000s, the logistical toil of scheduling five-day Tests - or later, eight-hour ODIs - had forced the ICC to suffer challenges aplenty: Olympic exclusion, empty stands on Test weekdays, and most importantly, a lack of new fans, who found it hard to get invested in a game demanding such immense temporal sacrifices.

Cricket had already established a stronghold in Commonwealth countries, but it was struggling to advance its borders.

Part of the problem was that generating interest in a sport and promoting club-level and grassroots-level cricket becomes far harder when you tell people that a typical match will take up their whole day. You could enjoy a football game, play a tennis match, and even round up your day with a basketball game, all while your mates at the cricket club still wouldn't be free from their first game!

In the age of Tiktok and social media, when YouTube Shorts, Instagram Reels, and bite-sized highlights are the best dopamine drip for our chronically-online youth and their goldfish-esque attention spans, cricket's longer formats simply weren't cut out for advancing the game. Leave the finances and logistics aside: if nobody's watching the game, what's the point of sport anymore?

These were the questions posed to the cricketing world at the dawn of the millennium. And once again - oddly reminiscent of the dawn of the 50-over game! - it was the ECB (England & Wales Cricket Board) who tested the waters.

Martin Crowe, the former Kiwi skipper known for his innovative captaincy and sharp cricketing mind, had proposed a new format for the sport in the mid-1990s: christened Cricket Max, he took inspiration from baseball to make cricket a game of four quarters, each consisting of ten eight-ball overs. While Cricket Max never made it outside local Kiwi cricketing circles, Stuart Robertson - the ECB's marketing manager - realised the necessity of a shorter format.

Remodelling Cricket Max to become a 20-overs-a-side game,

Robertson presented his proposal to the ECB. A groundbreaking motion to introduce the new format at a domestic level was passed 11-7 in his favour, and Twenty20 was born.

Little did they know the monster they had created!

At first, T20 remained a purely English affair. The first T20 domestic league was played in England in June 2003, and Robertson's booming marketing campaigns proved fruitful right from ball one: the first-ever T20 match, played between Middlesex and Surrey at Lord's, attracted 27,509 attendees - a massive sum! - setting a record for the highest attendance in any county game since 1953 according to the Guardian, finals excluded.

Other countries soon caught on, and Pakistan and Australia added these quickfire four-hour T20 tournaments to their domestic schedules. Being cheaper to host, drawing larger audiences, and occupying up a shorter span of time made the format perfect for recruiting domestic talent.

In 2005, Twenty20 cricket officially became the third international format: Australia and New Zealand played the first T20I. The affair was exciting and drew worldwide attention: Australia breached 200 straightaway, and the players donned retro kits in what was largely seen as a non-serious game. McGrath - when the Aussies' victory was imminent - hilariously recreated Trevor Chappell's infamous underarm bowling incident, for which the umpire Billy Bowden humorously punished him with a red card. All in all, the game was exciting, memorable, and - most importantly! - ended in three-and-a-half hours.

The ICC took advantage instantly: the first-ever T20 World Cup was organised in South Africa in 2007. A thrilling tournament featuring Yuvraj's six sixes, the India-Pakistan bowl-out, and several last-over nailbiters culminated in a dramatic clash between the perennial archrivals India and Pakistan - perhaps a foreshadowing of how the subcontinent would soon become the bastion of the shortest format.

The best thing the ICC could have hoped for was a thrilling final that made T20 cricket front-page news. And, boy did they get their heart's wish!

As Misbah tonked a six down the ground to bring the equation down to 6 off 4, the entire stadium - nay, the whole cricketing world! - stood electrified. The next ball rose up into the air - towards the shortest boundary - where Sreesanth took one of the most high-pressure catches in sporting history. India lifted the World Cup, redeeming the fiasco of their 2007 ODI campaign, and thus began the T20 boom in India - birthing the IPL the next year.

However, the influence of T20 extends far beyond this. As cricket began spreading in Afghanistan in the 2010s, it was the T20 format where they excelled. The reasons for this are several.

Firstly, being a shorter version of the game, it is far easier to promote, market, and recruit players for T20 cricket. Club players are far more willing to dedicate time to the game when they're sacrificing four hours a day rather than ten!

Secondly, being a shorter format, upsets are naturally more frequent. To win a Test, you need to be the better team for five straight days; to win a T20, all you need are 2-3 crucial moments to go your way. This was reflected in Afghanistan's momentous victory in the 2016 World T20 against the eventual champions West Indies, a win which massively boosted the importance of cricket in the region.

Thirdly, the ICC was able to use the T20 format to bring the 96 Associate members (as of 2024) out of hibernation.

While countries like Malawi and Vanuatu rarely had the monetary muscle to schedule a four-day first-class fixture or find the funds for a 50-over game, T20 matches were far more manageable - and simultaneously, far more viewer-friendly, crowd-friendly, and profitable.

It is, thus, no coincidence that the Netherlands' upset of South Africa in 2022, the USA's upset of Pakistan in 2024, and Namibia's upset of the Sri Lankans in 2022 - as well as countless other upsets - occurred not in ODI or Test cricket, but in the T20 format.

> ***"The ICC was able to use the T20 format to bring the Associate members out of hibernation."***

Fourthly, it allowed the ICC to grow the game: the 2021 and 2022 T20 World Cups featured 16 teams each, and the 2024 iteration was expanded to a hitherto-unprecedented 20 teams; by contrast, the 2019 ODI World Cup and the 2023 ODI World Cup were restricted to a comparatively-lowly figure of 10 teams. As the ICC now targets entry to the 2028 Olympics - a spectacle to which cricket's admission once seemed out of reach - it is the T20 format, the youngest child, which spearheads the charge.

Where, then, will this road lead on to?

The Abu Dhabi T10 League was launched by a Middle-Eastern billionaire, Nawab Shaji Ul Mulk, in 2018. The format further shortened T20 cricket into 10-overs-a-side matches, typically with flat batting-friendly pitches, to make the game even shorter, cheaper, and more profitable for investors. The ICC sanctioned it as a semi-professional league.

The ECB soon followed with the Hundred: an aptly-named hundred-ball-a-side competition designed to simplify cricket only into balls, runs, and wickets, thus making it marketable to an audience unaccustomed to overs, side changes, and the other technicalities of cricket. Soon, the Lanka T10 League, the Zim Afro League, and the Caribbean 6IXTY league all popped up, advertising ten-over cricket - is this cricket's future?

Is the ultimate fate of the most challenging of bat-ball sports nothing but to become a mere diluted, condensed, shrunken shadow of its once-glorious five-day form?

Is the inevitable fate of cricket - the slippery slope down which our sport is sliding - nothing but to become shorter and cheaper, swifter and quicker, and easier and more batting-friendly?

Is the ICC's newfound mission not preserving the sport, but filling their coffers gluttonously, endlessly, and insatiably?

The world of cricket teeters on the edge of a precipice. Money, franchise leagues, and new audiences tempt it towards dilution, while history, prestige, and nobility beckon it to uphold the established formats of the game.

The balanced path, however, appears to be the best.

The ICC should use T20s to make the big bucks needed to keep Test cricket alive and healthy. T20 games at the Olympics, T20 World Cups in the United States, and T20 games between Associates are the way to benefit cricket in the long run. At the same time, ODIs and Tests have their place: the ICC have wisely introduced the World Test Championship to keep Tests relevant, and the Cricket World Cup - played in the 50-over format - is still cricket's most esteemed trophy.

By using T20s to spread the game, the ICC cuts costs, prevents logistical headaches, and makes the game more accessible. After all, introducing someone to a four-hour-long sport with two innings is far easier than explaining the various intricacies and technicalities of Test cricket: declarations, follow-ons, nightwatchmen and what have you!

At the same time, the status of the oldest formats - in particular Test cricket - cannot be compromised.

Test cricket is, after all, still the pinnacle of the game.

The most fierce battles, the most-cherished rivalries, and the most thrilling finishes - Headingley 2019, Lord's 2021, Wellington 2023 - still happen in the Test format. There is no better sight in cricket than the final hour of the last session of the fifth day of a Test match when all three - or even four! - results are still on the cards. The suspense, the thrill, the anxiety - the game-changing potential of every delivery! - are all unparalleled.

However, that is not to say that the spectacle cannot be improved.

The vast disparity of the Test cricket calendar - with the Big Three playing nearly twice the number of Tests a year as the other nine Test-playing teams - is a major problem.

Sure, Test cricket doesn't fill the coffers as much as T20 cricket - but why can't the ICC use its T20-sourced profits to finance the existence of the five-day game?

"It's high time the governing body of world cricket showed some spine to rescue its oldest format."

Another problem which Test cricket is lacking, in my opinion, is the lack of India-Pakistan games. There is no doubt about it: India vs Pakistan is the premier rivalry of world cricket.

Do not forget that T20Is did not take off until India and Pakistan played two eternal classics in the 2007 World T20. And interestingly, even when one team has been far stronger than the other, these two have tended to produce utter classics time after time: the 2014 Asia Cup last-over clincher, the 2017 Champions

Trophy bounce-back, the back-to-back 2022 Asia Cup thrillers, the 2022 World Cup nailbiter, the 2024 World Cup thriller - the list is endless, even when the Indian team has been far stronger across formats in the last decade.

I am amazed that the ever-greedy ICC has not pounced on this opportunity. A neutral venue hosting a three-Test series - a possibility which both boards have publicly consented to! - would do wonders to revive Test cricket. Every session would have sold-out stands; every over would be cheered by packed stadiums; every match would set new records for broadcasting statistics. And yet, the ICC remains unambitious.

"Test cricket is, after all, still the pinnacle of the game."

The ICC, as the custodians of the game, have the honour and the burden of preserving all three formats of the game. However, the World Test Championship introduced in 2019 is, in its current state, an absolute abomination.

Position	Team	Played	W	L	Draw	PCT	Points
1	IND	9	6	2	1	68.51	74
2	AUS	12	8	3	1	62.50	90
3	NZ	6	3	3	0	50.00	36
4	SL	4	2	2	0	50.00	24
5	SA	6	2	3	1	38.89	28
6	PAK	5	2	3	0	36.66	22
7	ENG	13	6	6	1	36.54	57
8	BAN	4	1	3	0	25.00	12
9	WI	9	1	6	2	18.52	20

The World Test Championship table as of August 18th, 2024.

Look at the table above: one competitor has played 13 matches, while another has played 4! Another team with 57 points is, bizarrely, ranked below a team with 22! How can this tournament possibly be used to grow interest in the red-ball game? What use is a points table when you need a degree in higher mathematics to explain it to a casual watcher?

The WTC has limitless potential, but it is a joke in its current state.

A true league-style Test cricket championship can only function if the ICC wakes up the Future Tours Programme (FTP). The fact that bilateral series are organised, negotiated, and scheduled between cricket boards without the ICC's direct control is the root of the FTP's problems.

The ICC needs to have direct input in series scheduling. Every country should be made to play a Test series with each other team over a period of three years: there's only twelve Test-playing teams, surely this is the bare minimum! I see no reason why this can't be done if the ICC takes charge of the matter. Let all boards agree to it, or else face sanctions. It's high time the governing body of world cricket showed some spine to rescue its oldest format.

A WTC where all teams play each other would not only create an incentive for teams to invest time and money into Test cricket, but it would give purpose to each game: rather than Bangladesh and Pakistan playing for a meaningless "Blue World City Test Series Trophy 2024", they would be fighting for qualification in a global championship. If bonus points are introduced for winning with a certain margin, every run would become a dogfight for points - adding context to a sport that lacks it.

I further propose that the ICC should have absolutely no problem expanding the WTC to have a semi-finals based system. The thrill of knock-out matches with a trophy on the line is unmatched in all of sport: logistically, it won't take longer than two weeks to play two simultaneous five-day semi-finals and another five-day final with a four-day break in between - an easy opportunity to grow the game that the ICC neglects.

> ***"What use is a points table when you need a degree in higher mathematics to explain it to a casual watcher?"***

In any case, it is the responsibility of the custodians of the game to preserve all three formats.

Each format has its grandeur - Tests for history and prestige, ODIs for the biggest trophy in world cricket, T20s to grow the game and attract new fans - and I, for one, am nothing but utterly grateful for the three unique formats - each with its own idiosyncrasies! - that we are blessed to enjoy.

Franchise Leagues: A New World Order?

In 1945, the five most powerful countries of the world - Russia, China, the UK, the USA, and France - sat down to form the United Nations and establish a new world order. In cricket, a similar struggle lies right before our eyes.

The question is fundamental in nature: what gives the ICC the right to govern world cricket and harvest all its profits? The answer: nothing at all.

The ICC only enjoys the right to rule because all the major national boards recognise it as a suitable governing body and negotiating platform - after all, how would cricket thrive if nobody could agree on which rules to use and which events to participate in? Ensuring fairness, justice, and uniformity across all professional cricket matches is the core responsibility of the ICC.

But - as Kerry Packer proved in 1977 - with the right ideas and right tools at the right time, the hegemony could be unravelled remarkably quickly.

Our tale begins in 2007, when the ICL was launched in India. Nope, that's not a typo: not the IPL, but rather, a rebel league christened the ICL (Indian Cricket League).

With the advent of the T20 format, the logistical burden of cricket eased immensely. Rather than hiring broadcasters, commentators, umpires, ball-boys, security personnel, transport facilities, and cameramen for five long days or even for ten long hours, all of a sudden cricket became a four-hour affair. This cut the costs massively, while simultaneously increasing the profits exponentially, as more crowds began filling stadiums and more casual fans found it feasible to follow four-hour T20s rather than week-long Tests.

The real T20 revolution was not sporting, but financial.

In 2007, following India's surprising World T20 triumph - and surprising it was indeed, as nearly all their senior players had opted out of the tournament - Zee Entertainment Enterprises, a local media giant, reached the same realisation.

Swiftly recruiting nine city-based franchise teams - seven Indian cities, one Bangladeshi, and one even Pakistani! - they launched the Indian Cricket League - again, just like Packer's WSC, a rebel league: one unsanctioned by the BCCI, unrecognized by the ICC, and unprecedented in its scope.

This ICL was the world's first franchise league. Promising players and coaches high salaries, they recruited some of the world's leading stars, including ex-cricketers Inzamam-ul-Haq, Moin Khan, and Kiran More, as well as the superstar Kapil Dev in a supervisory role. They set new trends, notably assigning a mentor and sports psychologist to each team - a forward-thinking philosophy. Many contemporary players joined as well - prominent among them were the young Indian stars in the making: Ambati Rayudu, Stuart Binny, and Sunil Gavaskar's son, Rohan. Tempted by cash and perhaps impressed by the tournament's revolutionary new ideas to transform T20 cricket, they took a giant leap into the unknown.

"The real T20 revolution was not sporting, but financial."

While the ICL perhaps failed to reach the heights of the WSC before it or the IPL after it, its impact cannot be underestimated. After all, they were the first league in history to adopt a franchise system: even the WSC had been based on nationalities.

The BCCI took this threat seriously, and boycotted the ICL and took them to court. The ICL administration, however, came prepared: winning the court case in the Delhi High Court.

This sent the BCCI into a panic, who had realised the immense financial potential of the ICL. If the ICL got hold of more cricketers, there was nothing stopping it from toppling the BCCI and ICC at the top of world cricket's pyramid.

The BCCI responded by raising domestic players' salaries and prize money amounts - doubling them in some cases, and increasing them even more in others. This was done to dissuade players from being tempted by the ICL's main incentive: money.

Furthermore, the BCCI threatened to boycott any player found playing in the ICL. This, naturally, was a threat the players took far more seriously.

The ICL, for its part, found success with its franchise league model; thereafter, it decided to take on the ICC as well in cricket's equivalent of a World War. Organising international matches between "ICL India", "ICL Pakistan", and "ICL Bangladesh" - comprised of very strong teams studded with each nation's superstars - the ICL began to gain momentum.

However, the BCCI's sanctions - coupled with the ICL's own logistical problems that started to creep in - as well as the BCCI's efforts to increase domestic salaries and offer amnesty to players who agreed to boycott the ICL, eventually quelled the rebellion.

Though the ICL died down, the idea remained alive: a football-esque or NBA-esque franchise-based model could not only survive, but thrive in the world of cricket.

It was the BCCI who now pounced on the opportunity.

In 2008, the IPL was created, the brainchild of Lalit Modi - the Vice-President of the BCCI at the time. Inspired largely by the rebel ICL, the IPL was to have eight city-based franchises. An auction would determine which team got which player, and after a double-round-robin league stage, the playoffs would culminate in a grand final.

Little did they know that this tournament would define cricket for the next generation!

The BCCI took several bold risks with this plan of the IPL.

Firstly, the decision to have a player auction seemed, at the time, to be a reasonable one, but later turned out to be a marketing masterclass. The entertainment, suspense, and anxiety of the auction, as well as the inter-team trades and transfers, essentially became an event in its own right. It would not be inaccurate to say that the IPL Auction Day is watched nearly as fanatically by cricket followers as the IPL Final.

Apart from this, the auction system also provides a fairly-meritocratic basis for determining player salaries, while simultaneously allowing the best players to reap gigantic rewards: in the first ever auction, MS Dhoni stole the show when the Chennai-based franchise purchased his services for the whopping sum of USD 1.5 million.

Secondly, the calendar slot of the IPL was also a headache for the BCCI. The first edition of the competition was one-and-a-half month long: as long as a World Cup or an Ashes series. It was now counting on the players' desire for money to overcome their desire to play for their national teams for 44 days: a massive ask at the time. Moreover, the timing of the IPL was - and still is - April/May, when fixtures of all formats are being played all across the world.

However, money talks, and when the player salaries came to light after the first auction, all the players suddenly found themselves rushing to make time for the IPL.

In the current cricketing climate, April/May has essentially become a dedicated IPL window. World Cups, other leagues, and bilateral series all take an off-season for two months, while the cricketing fraternity assembles in India for an extravaganza of sport.

However, Pakistan remains sidelined for these two months, as the Indian government aims to isolate their archenemy in both sports and geopolitics. It is a pity, for I believe that politics should have no place in sports, and the Pakistani players lit up the 2008 IPL with their brilliant performances - Sohail Tanvir bagging the best figures of the IPL with his spell of 6/14 - but the political overlords of our world fail to relent.

In any case, the world assembled in India in 2008 for a giant experiment of cricket. Would it succeed, or would it fall flat?

On the 18th of April, 2008, the Kolkata Knight Riders' openers strode out to meet the Royal Challengers Bangalore after an ostentatious opening ceremony in front of a jam-packed Chinnaswamy Stadium. T20 strategies were still antique and unclear; data analytics was hardly heard of; chasing 40 off 30 still seemed to be a tall order.

Brendon McCullum, though, had other ideas.

Bashing the bowlers to all parks of the ground en route his 158* (73), he immediately set the tone for the IPL in the first innings itself. An exhilarating, breathtaking, and action-packed innings rose to a crescendo after a slow start and kept the crowd entertained. Pushing the pedal to the metal, he never took his foot off the accelerator, and the crowd gasped in awe as they saw the IPL burst out of its cocoon before their eyes.

Before long, the IPL sent the cricketing world into a frenzy. Fans all over the globe found themselves cheering for cities they had never visited - an unheard-of phenomenon. Ticket sales burst through the roof and the IPL's broadcasting deals were soon making shockwaves in the entire world of sport: the IPL was truly alive and kicking.

A thrilling final was all it needed, and when Shane Warne's Rajasthan outfit triumphed over the Dhoni-led Chennai Super Kings on the very final ball of the tournament, the world of cricket would never be the same again.

For one, the franchise system had truly worked: before the tournament, one of the key worries of organisers was how players of different teams would gel together in such a short span of time. Not just the players, but the coaching staff, the owners, the physiotherapists, the data analysts, and a host of other staff-members would all have to establish their team chemistry within two or three weeks! Sure, World XIs had played one-off games before, but back in 2008, the franchise model was a leap of faith into the unknown.

However, the players displayed maturity and gelled together surprisingly well; indeed, the iconic image of Shoaib Akhtar, the Pakistani express pace bowler, hugging the Bollywood icon Shahrukh Khan after an IPL victory summed up the uniting spirit of the IPL. A decade later in the 2019 edition, Jonny Bairstow of England and David Warner of Australia hugged it out on the pitch as they both notched up their centuries - and to think this happened in an Ashes year!

The global corporate valuation firm, Brand Finance, values the IPL at an estimated USD 10.7 billion - an unimaginable sum. In 2017, the broadcasting rights of the IPL for the next five years were sold to the Star India network for USD 2.55 billion - another tremendous figure.

Seeing the rise of the IPL, other cricketing boards decided to join the fun.

The Australian Big Bash League was established in 2011, and they went a step further and introduced a Women's Big Bash League five years down the line. The Bangladesh Premier League, Pakistan Super League, and Caribbean Premier League soon followed, and before long, every nation had its own cheap copy of the IPL.

This begs the question that the ICC is still trying to answer: how can all these franchise leagues - more than a dozen now! - exist in tandem with the international calendar?

Till today, nobody has been able to answer this question.

As the BCCI continues to take the IPL from strength to strength - expanding to ten teams in 2022 and planning further expansions - the ICC fears for international cricket. Is the day near when the cricket calendar will simply consist of one franchise league after another?

To further stir the pot, the BCCI is indirectly the ICC's primary financier. India's cricket-crazy population of a billion viewers is its biggest asset: the sky-high viewership numbers being the ICC's primary argument to persuade broadcasters to bid for lucrative deals.

This makes it awkward for the ICC to go head-to-head with the

BCCI, knowing that if the ICC loses its Indian asset, its coffers will remain empty.

Another problem is the lack of coordination between boards. While the ICC can coordinate the Future Tours Programme to manage bilateral series between member nations, there is no such board between franchise leagues. What is stopping the PSL and BBL from clashing with the IPL's window? Or indeed, what if every league occupies a separate window in the calendar, thus eclipsing international cricket as franchise leagues become a year-round presence? Even worse, what if leagues not affiliated with any Test nation - such as Major League Cricket in the USA or the Abu Dhabi T10 League - dare to clash with an ICC event? Will the World Cup be diluted by these franchise leagues?

Soon, players realised that by getting lucrative deals from franchise leagues all over the world, one could earn far more than any country's central contract could offer.

"This begs the question that the ICC is still trying to answer: how can all these franchise leagues - more than a dozen now! - exist in tandem with the international calendar?"

Kieron Pollard was the first to pounce, becoming cricket's first "freelancer". Cameron Delport, Sunil Narine, and Dan Christian soon followed, and they began earning more than their patriotic counterparts.

The concept of mercenary cricketers threatens the foundations of international cricket. Why, if players are content to play for anyone putting a stack of cash on the table - patriotic loyalty notwithstanding - what legs will international sport have left to stand on?

These questions remain unanswered by the ICC. However, time is running out.

The ICC's response, it seems, has been to keep international cricket relevant by increasing the number and frequency of ICC events. The World Test Championship was launched, the Champions Trophy was reinstated, and the frequency of T20 World Cups was increased - all measures aimed at preventing the new world order of franchise leagues from taking over.

Furthermore, the move to make cricket a permanent addition to the Olympics is, in my opinion, merely another attempt by the ICC to keep the international game alive. After all, if players and boards have a World Cup to compete for every year, and the Olympics every once in a while, surely it will delay the rise of the new world order?

Another challenge for the ICC has been ensuring the sport of cricket's reputation does not suffer in these leagues, which unfortunately have become rife with betting scandals and spot-fixing controversies. Being much harder to police due to their short duration, massive popularity, and the number of different leagues across the globe, several spot-fixing scandals have brought the sport into disrepute - notably the IPL spot-fixing scandal of 2013.

While the number of fixing cases in international cricket have massively declined since the establishment of the ICC's Anti-Corruption Unit in 2000, the governing body fears a resurgence may occur in these franchise leagues, where culprits are far harder to catch and due punishments more difficult to execute.

Another challenge the ICC faces is a dilution of the rules of the game. The minimum boundary length ordained by the ICC, 59 metres, is often ignored by IPL officials to create high-scoring showdowns. Sunil Narine, the West Indian spinner whose action has often been deemed illegal by the ICC, opts to play only franchise leagues rather than international cricket, knowing that the implementation of the 15-degree-rule is far more lenient in franchise leagues. And of course, the ECB's Hundred completely threw the rulebook out of the window, getting rid of overs and making cricket a hundred-balls-a-side affair.

All these infringements weaken the ICC's status as the lawmaker and custodian of the game.

In 2023, the BCCI introduced the *Impact Player* rule in the IPL, allowing teams to substitute a player off the bench into the playing XI during the game.

This football-esque or basketball-esque idea had no precedent in cricket. The ICC or the MCC had never sanctioned it. The Laws of Cricket did not condone it. And yet, the ICC was powerless to stop franchise leagues from changing the fabric of the game: threatening the very concept of all-rounders and catalysing a massive upturn in batting totals.

The *Impact Player* rule is a minor rule, but it depicts the ICC's helplessness. What if a franchise league tomorrow permits underarm bowling? Or what if another franchise league starts awarding ten runs for balls that soar over the boundary? Or another league allows fifteen players per side? Even worse, what if each league starts having its own rules without uniformity between them? Oh, wait - that's already happening, as the Hundred and the IPL have several notable differences.

The ICC needs to step in and demand all national boards to allow the ICC to directly govern the play, the rules, and the Laws of their franchise leagues - or else, the world of cricket will soon be split into a thousand different leagues with a thousand different rulebooks. If every league continues to put its own twist onto cricket, then this begs the question: at what point is it no longer cricket?

Furthermore, franchise leagues allow the revenue to go directly to the hands of national cricketing boards, where the money more often tends to fill the private coffers of the overlords rather than get invested to improve the sport. By contrast, all revenue from ICC events goes directly to the ICC, who can then supervise how the money is used and develop Associate cricket and grassroots cricket through it.

The rise of franchise leagues makes the trail of money far murkier, and less and less profits are poured into Associate cricket.

> ***"What if a franchise league tomorrow permits underarm bowling? Or another franchise league starts awarding ten runs for balls that soar over the boundary? Or another league allows fifteen players per side?"***

Cricket tragics fear the parallel with football, a sport where the modern calendar is now dominated by city-based franchise leagues - the English Premier League, La Liga, Bundesliga, you name it - or with basketball, where the most-followed event is the American NBA, whilst the official FIBA World Cup remains relatively obscure. The rise of franchise leagues threatens the existence of international cricket as we know it.

However, the positives also exist: Associate cricketers making a name by performing in franchise leagues, a la Sandeep Lamichhane of Nepal; freelancing cricketers being able to provide for their families by earning more in franchise league auctions; national boards being able to gather funds needed to host ICC events and bilateral series via these lucrative leagues, and so on.

Nonetheless, the ICC needs to prevent the potential problems of franchise leagues from upending the world order of cricket. The biggest nightmare of the ICC is the emergence of a rival body that eclipses the ICC in its scope and power - and currently, the IPL looks set to oust international cricket one day, if it continues expanding at its current rate. There are some steps the ICC must urgently take before it no longer has any respite.

Firstly, it is imperative to establish a clear calendar for franchise leagues. Either restrict all franchise leagues to be played in a certain window of the calendar - say the first four months of the year - and reserve the rest for international cricket, or else assign each league its own unique window when no other league will be permitted to clash with it.

Secondly, a joint committee must be formed - led by the ICC's Anti-Corruption Unit - to oversee, pre-empt, and prevent fixing scandals from occurring. Moreover, the committee should also allow the ICC to ensure the Laws of the game are properly upheld in each league: the boundary lengths, bowling actions, and sporting regulations should be enforced uniformly.

"If every league continues to put its own twist onto cricket, then this begs the question: at what point is cricket no longer cricket?"

Moreover, financial accountability is also necessary. The profits and budgets of each league need to be monitored, and each league should be required to invest a certain amount of its profits - say, 15% - into developing Associate cricket or grassroots cricket. Mandating one Associate player to be a part of every squad in each league would also be a commendable step.

Additionally, the ICC needs to co-operate with the leagues. As the saying goes: "If you can't beat 'em, join 'em." There is no reason - yet! - for the ICC to be openly at war with these leagues. If they play their cards smartly, they can form an umbrella commission to coordinate between all cricket leagues under the mandate of the ICC. With luck, such an organisation would also be able to resurrect the idea of a Champions League: an annual super-tournament to be held between the champion teams of each league!

If football can successfully conduct a Champions League - possibly the single biggest football tournament outside of the World Cup - why can't cricket?

Although the BCCI, Cricket Australia, and Cricket South Africa tried to launch a Champions League that ran on-and-off from 2008 to 2014, it soon failed due to logistical issues. However, if such a competition were to be held with the approval, assistance, and cooperation of the ICC, I have no doubt that it would be a massive success, and an immensely positive addition to the cricketing calendar.

In any case, the sheer impact of the franchise league model - pioneered by Kerry Packer, resurrected by the ICL, and perfected by the IPL - has changed cricket the way we know it.

After all, who could ever have imagined that one day, the words "player auction", "transfer window", and "Mumbai Indians New York" would be part of the cricketing dictionary?

Epilogue: A New Dawn

Cricket is one of the world's oldest extant sports, with its professional history dating back to 1877.

Yet, when I finished writing this book, it struck me that four of the Ten Moments That Changed Cricket occurred in the last twenty years alone. Indeed, the rate of change of the sport in the 21st century - powered by a mixture of technology, capitalism, and innovation - is nothing short of unprecedented.

However, the sport stands on the edge of a precipice.

Is it time, then, to embrace the US market - the final frontier - and make short-form cricket the face of the sport? Say, T10, or - even more egregiously - F5?

Or are there still those who spend sleepless nights watching away Test matches, their heart beating faster and breath becoming quicker and goosebumps rising as the target becomes closer? Those who celebrate every win with passion, and mourn every heartbreak with tears - anger, even, at times, coupled with frustration - yet still relentlessly tune in for the next day's game? Those for whom cricket is not just a sport to watch, but a series of mental calculations going on in their head as they gaze, engrossed, at the match: should the skipper declare with a lead of 280, or bat another session?

If these fans still exist, and if - dear reader! - you are one of them, then I have no fear for the world of cricket. For it is the fans who are the soul of the sport, for whom the cricketers and administrators and broadcasters and umpires and commentators and cameramen and ball-boys toil with their blood, sweat, and tears: it is you, the fans, who make every win worth celebrating, and every loss worth mourning. Oh, what is the worth of a World Cup trophy - a mere lump of brass and gold! - except that it carries within it a nation's hopes, fears, and passions?

Predicting the future is a fool's errand, especially when the sport being discussed is one as rapidly-evolving and volatile as our beloved game. Nonetheless, it behoves me, dear reader, to leave you with some thoughts on where the sport might head from here.

Firstly, I do not believe international cricket will be killed off easily - not without a fight. Indeed, the international format of our game is far more entrenched in history than it ever was in football, basketball, or soccer. While I foresee T20 leagues - led by the financial behemoth that is the IPL - expanding steadily, I do not see bilateral series dying out within the next couple of decades, nor do I envision any reduction in the number of ICC events.

I do, however, expect - and even hope for! - the formation of a Champions League. Not the sham that the 2008-14 fiasco was - but a proper, ICC-affiliated, thoroughly-coordinated Champions League. If our cricketing overlords truly want to fill their coffers with gold, a potential Champions League is nothing but a goldmine lying in wait.

As for the ICC's attempts to spread the game, I do expect the T20 World Cup to become a 24-team or even a 30-team affair within the next two decades. The crucial lesson cricket must remember is: let them be uncompetitive at first! Afghanistan did not demolish Full Members straight out of the gate, nor did Pakistan before it, nor did New Zealand or South Africa before it. Let the new teams join the cricketing fraternity slowly and steadily! Losing by a hundred runs - or more - is perfectly acceptable: not being included in a World Cup isn't.

I view the decision to make cricket a part of the Olympics in an extremely positive light: regardless of the format, it is imperative for the survival of international cricket. Let franchise leagues rule the world! But whenever the time for an Olympics edition arrives nigh, the dormant patriotism in every cricketer will be bound to waken, and international cricket will thus continue to thrive.

The World Test Championship is undoubtedly a flawed tournament - surely the massive disparity in the number of matches played by each team is alarming! - but neither was the 1975 World Cup perfect, and even the 1992 edition had a rain-rule fiasco, and even the 2019 iteration had a controversial end. Never chase perfectionism; the WTC is a good start, and it provides every team an incentive to play a format for which the monetary incentive is essentially nil.

I do not, however, agree with the longstanding notion of "Test status" being restricted to twelve nations.

Let the Associates play Test cricket if they so wish! If a team of American cricketers wishes to play a five-day game with England, there should be no problem if both boards agree. Why does their historical significance to the ICC matter? Again, gatekeeping the sport is a dangerous path to tread: opening the doors to all three formats, while prioritising the shortest ones for Associates, is the wisest path.

The format I fear most for, however, is ODI cricket - indeed, the format which has suffered the most post-pandemic. The stark decrease in the number of ODI matches - not long ago the most frequently-played format! - is worthy of attention; as a lover of the ODI game and someone who truly believes it to be the most balanced of the sport's three formats, I call upon the ICC to create further incentives for ODI cricket. The decision to abolish the Champions' Trophy was a disaster; I am glad it has been revoked.

Speaking of the Champions' Trophy, the 2025 edition is bound to be interesting - not least the fact that India, the ICC's financial cow, will doubtless be unwilling to travel to Pakistan. I am hopeful that one day, political tensions between the two countries will stop affecting sporting fixtures; however, that day has not come yet.

Whether India travels to Pakistan or not, and how Pakistan reacts to it, will be a very key moment in their cricketing relationship. The ICC - and both boards - know how much money they are missing out on by not touring one another. Indeed, I often remark that what Test cricket really needs for its revival is an exciting India vs Pakistan series; however, I am confident that whenever the day comes when the BCCI or the ICC are in need of a quick cash-grab, they will promptly orchestrate an India vs Pakistan series again, in all likelihood at a neutral venue. Were the ICC to be more forward-thinking, it would mandate an Ashes-esque Test series to be played between both countries via the Future Tours Programme; alas, it is us cricket fans who suffer from the ICC's incompetence.

In any case, dear reader, the sport of cricket is very much alive and kicking - and changing.

Ten crucial moments have changed the game before us: from the origins of the Ashes to the establishment of franchise leagues. However, countless revolutionary moments lie ahead - the potential for growth and destruction, both, exists.

It is not, however, the ICC that truly "governs" cricket. It is the fans - and the same applies to any sport.

While there are still eight-year-olds at school who copy Jasprit Bumrah's action between lessons - and adults who will still, occasionally, break into a slingy Malinga yorker when walking down an empty corridor - our sport will thrive. While there are still clubs and fields populated with budding players day in and day out - our sport will thrive. And while there are still elderly gentlemen, sitting in clubs and reminiscing about Sobers' 365* and Gooch's 333 - our sport will thrive.

Long live cricket.

Picture Source Links

49a   https://www.thesun.co.uk/wp-content/uploads/2019/08/
NINTCHDBPICT000509979950.jpg?strip
=all&quality=100&w=1920&h=1080&crop=1 - The Sun

49b   https://artsandculture.google.com/asset/original-ashes-obituary-the-
sporting-times-london/FAGF
nRPLrlgFNQ?hl=en - Google Arts and Culture

50a   https://en.wikipedia.org/wiki/W._G._Grace

50b   https://www.thecricketmonthly.com/story/885241/the-greatest-ashes-test

51a   https://www.gettyimages.in/photos/don-bradman

51b   https://www.pinterest.co.uk/pin/don-bradman-
australia--718535315542973791/

52a   https://www.sportsboom.com/cricket/world-cup/1975-cricket-world-cup/

52b   https://www.sportphotogallery.com/cricket/ashes-2019/

53   https://www.gettyimages.ca/detail/news-photo/world-series-cricket-
sydney-1979-australia-v-west-indies-news-photo/160643366   -   Getty
Images

54a   https://www.linkedin.com/pulse/success-breeds-other-corporate-
lessons-from-indias-triumph-bhatt

54b   https://www.gettyimages.com/photos/imran-khan-1992

55a   https://www.espncricinfo.com/story/javed-miandad-on-sharjah-1986-to-
describe-it-is-impossiblethis-was-a-gift-from-god-1259275

55b   https://niravkhanal.com.np/cricket/the-day-greed-killed-cricket/kishor_
nirav54/

56a https://www.gettyimages.ca/detail/news-photo/world-series-cricket-administrator-kerry-packer-and-england-news-photo/1074404890   -
Getty Images

56b https://www.independent.co.uk/news/obituaries/tony-lewis-death-cricket-duckworth-method-agecause-mathetmatics-a9464921.html

57a https://www.thecricketmonthly.com/story/1402019/the-maximum-game

57b https://www.espncricinfo.com/story/what-we-remember-south-africa-chasing-australia-s-434-in-johannesburg-2006-1139063

58a https://medium.com/rario/innovations-in-cricket-decision-review-system-drs-3181f02726cc

58b   https://www.foxsports.com.au/cricket/australia/closeup-of-drs-decision-after-steve-smith-lbw-appeal-reveals-frightening-error/news-story/9908283d5af9731a571448b0044de6ed

59   https://www.espncricinfo.com/story/the-greatest-ipl-performances-no-3-chris-gayle-175-not-out-and-2-for-5-vs-the-pune-warriors-1258705

60a https://tilomitra.com/analyzing-tendulkars-batting/

60b https://www.indiatoday.in/sports/cricket/story/ipl-2024-gt-vs-srh-heinrich-klaasen-form-2521424-2024-03-31

61a https://olympics.com/en/news/first-t20-cricket-match

61b https://www.mid-day.com/sports/cricket/article/ipl-auction-2024-what-will-the-teams-look-forward-to-23325539

62a https://www.sportskeeda.com/cricket/ipl-2018-why-franchisees-likely-retain-2-rather-than-3-players

62b https://cricketpakistan.com.pk/en/news/detail/hbl-psl-8-heres-the-list-of-players-participating-in-exhibition-match

63   https://twitter.com/t10league

64a https://www.gettyimages.ca/detail/news-photo/the-boston-celtics-raise-2008-world-championship-banner-news-photo/83470703

64b https://www.forbes.com/sites/manasipathak-1/2023/10/03/odi-cricket-should-be-played-only-at-world-cups-says-mcc-president/

* 9 7 8 9 6 9 0 0 2 9 2 9 4 *